THE BORDER VALE
OF GLAMORGAN

*The author and publisher wish to
express their gratitude to the
following individuals, firms and
organisations who have kindly
sponsored this book*

Bayswater Tubes & Sections Ltd., Pencoed
Burridge Construction Co. Ltd., Forestwood, Llantrisant
P. Gwyn Humphrey & Son Ltd., Llanharan
Councillor Harry Lewis, Chairman, Llanharry Community Council
Llanharry Community Council
Llanharry Commoners' Association
Maxihet (Anthracite Briquettes) Ltd., Mwyndy Mills, Llantrisant
J. & L. Perriam, Haulage Contractors, Aberkenfig
Malcolm Powell, Llanharry
Staedtler (U.K.) Ltd., Pontyclun
K. B. Thomas, B.A., J.P., Principal, Coleg y Fro, YMCA Training
    College, Rhoose
Miss Mair E. Thomas, Gilfach Goch
Y Pant School Parents' Association Trust Fund, Talbot Green

THE BORDER VALE
OF
GLAMORGAN

David J. Francis

Photographs by
Haydn Baynham

STEWART WILLIAMS, PUBLISHERS
BARRY, SOUTH GLAMORGAN

First Published 1976

ISBN 0 900807 22 9

Introduction

Since contributing articles to *Glamorgan Historian* I have always nursed an ambition to write a full-length book of my own about the Border Vale. I would therefore at the outset like to thank my publisher Stewart Williams for giving me this unique opportunity to do so. I am also deeply grateful to my friend Brian Ll. James of University College Library, Cardiff, whose guidance and knowledge have been of inestimable value. Another friend Roy Denning has given me helpful advice on numerous occasions. I also owe a special debt of gratitude to Haydn Baynham of Cardiff whose photographs are such an attractive feature of this book.

Acknowledgments are due to the National Portrait Gallery, National Museum of Wales, and the National Library of Wales, for allowing me to reproduce their prints. My thanks also to Robert Williams for the excellent map of the Border Vale. I also wish to thank Dr. H. N. Savory, Keeper of the Department of Archaeology at the National Museum of Wales, and the staffs of the Royal Commission on Ancient and Historical Monuments in Wales, Cardiff Central Library, Mid Glamorgan County Library, Bridgend, and Glamorgan Archive Service for help freely given. A word of thanks also to Dewi Jones of Pontyclun for his guidance on photographic material, and to all those kind people who loaned me a large number of photographs during my researches. I have been very fortunate indeed in having so many patrons and sponsors and I would like to record my appreciation of their generosity.

At a local level I wish to thank Councillor Harry Lewis for his advice on mining, Mark N. Powell of Pantyquesta, Graham Rees of Aberkenfig, Mrs. Nancy Aston of Pontyclun, and my headmaster, William Brydle of Llanharry. Also I would like to convey my warmest thanks to Gwyn Evans and his Book Committee who have worked tirelessly on my behalf. I am grateful to those people in the district — too numerous to mention — who have helped in one form or another. And lastly a word of thanks to my typists Mrs. Sybil Jones, Mrs. Janet Morgan and Miss Linda Beach.

Llanharry   DAVID J. FRANCIS

The Border Vale Book Committee

Seated: (left to right) — Miss Angela Harris, Mrs. Sybil J. Jones, Mrs. Janet Morgan, Mrs. Maureen Pring, Miss Rhonda Demmer, Mrs. Yvonne Eley, Mrs. Fleur Thomas.

Standing: (left to right) — John Smith, William Urquhart, David Thomas, Councillor Harry Lewis, Gordon Cattell, Stan Welsh, Gwyn Evans (Chairman) and John Andrews.

Other members: Paul and Christine Sanders, Steve Evans, Colin Smith and Councillor Ivor J. B. Williams.

THE BORDER VALE

BROADLY speaking, the Border Vale is the tract of transitional country lying between the low plateau of the Vale of Glamorgan and the high plateau of the uplands, commonly called the Blaenau. It is bounded by the River Ely on the east, the common portway (A48) on the south, the River Ewenny on the west, and the steep escarpment of the coalfields on the north. Belonging to this region are the parishes of Pendoylan, Welsh St. Donats, Ystradowen, Llanharry, Llansannor, Llanilid, St. Mary Hill, Llangan and most of Penllyn. The southern parts of Peterston-super-Montem, Llanharan and Llantrisant are included, as is the northern portion of Llanblethian. I have also included the modern township of Pencoed in my account owing to its proximity to the River Ewenny.

From earliest times the people of the Border Vale have not regarded themselves as 'men of the Vale'. To them the land south of the A48 is a separate region. As early as 1578, William Camden,

Pysgodlyn   Photograph: Haydn Baynham

an Elizabethan antiquary, anticipated the modern concept of a transitional zone — or Border Vale — lying between the Vale and the uplands of Glamorgan. 'On the north', he wrote, 'it is very rugged with mountains, which inclining towards the south become by degrees more tillable, at the roots whereof we have a spacious Vale or plain open to the South Sun . . . For this part of the County is exceeding pleasant, both in regard to the fertility of the soil and the number of towns and villages'.

Basically, the region is bounded from the Vale of Glamorgan by a series of low, limestone hills which run roughly in an east-west direction from Stallingdown to the River Ewenny. To the north of these Downlands between the Thaw and the Ely valleys lies the broad undulating basin sometimes called Bro Miskin. Much of this basin is covered by a thick mantle of glacial drift, which was deposited by the coalescence of ice tongues from Irish Sea and upland sources during the Ice Age. Occasionally, 'islands' of carboniferous and other rocks project out of the covering of drift, as at Llanharry. However, the terrain of much of the Border Vale is hummocky and has a 'kame and kettle' appearance.

One of the most important characteristics of this well defined region is the uneven fertility of the soils. The Border Vale has been noted for its large number of commons and rough pasture, some of which like Morfa Ystradowen and Llanharry Meadow still remain uncultivated. The Llangan district, however, while it in part contains open limestone downland, has its fair share of good agricultural land, and it was no accident that the Normans established their corn growing manors at Penllyn, Goston and Llangan. Elsewhere, on the glacial drift, the distinction between areas of freely drained and impeded soils is fundamental to the understanding of the history of the whole region. On a narrow tract of land from Aberthin to Llanharry, the freely drained loams have been cultivated from earliest times. But elsewhere, especially in the northern and eastern parts of the Border Vale, we have to envisage a landscape where through much of the past trees were thicker on the ground than people. Even today in driving off the A48 towards Pendoylan one is struck by the dramatic change in the scenery. One leaves the fertile Vale and passes immediately into a forested area.

It can also be shown that the Border Vale is a transitional zone between the Vale and the Blaenau in settlement pattern and economy. The Vale has always been a countryside of small, compact parishes, nucleated villages and a farming economy with much emphasis on corn growing. In the Border Vale, by contrast, there has always been less arable and more meadowland. Given the pastoral and wooded nature of much of the area, it is hardly

8

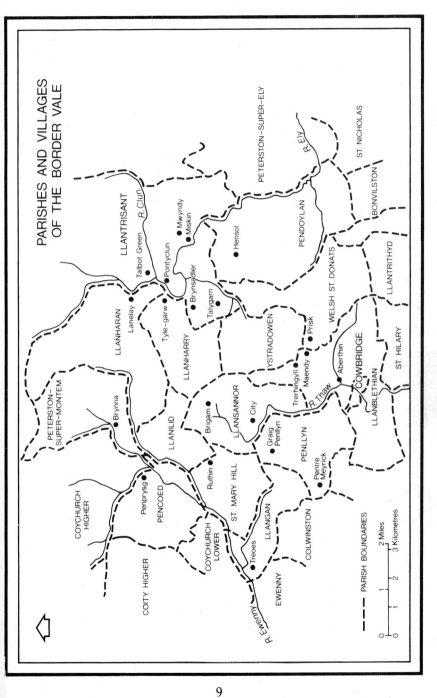

PARISHES AND VILLAGES
OF THE BORDER VALE

LLANTRISANT
R. Clun
Talbot Green
Pontyclun
Mwyndy
Miskin
Brynsadler
Hensol
PETERSTON-SUPER-ELY
R. Ely
PENDOYLAN
ST. NICHOLAS
BONVILSTON
LLANTRITHYD
LLANHARAN
Lanelay
Tyle-garw
Talygarn
LLANHARRY
YSTRADOWEN
Prisk
WELSH ST. DONATS
Maendy
Trerhingyll
Aberthin
COWBRIDGE
ST. HILARY
PETERSTON-
SUPER-MONTEM
Brynna
LLANILID
Brigam
LLANSANNOR
City
Graig
Penllyn
R. Thaw
PENLLYN
LLANBLETHIAN
COYCHURCH
HIGHER
Penprysg
PENCOED
Ruthin
ST. MARY HILL
Pentre
Meyrick
COITY HIGHER
COYCHURCH
LOWER
LLANGAN
COLWINSTON
Treoes
EWENNY
R. Ewenny

- - - PARISH BOUNDARIES

0   1   2 Miles
0   1   2   3 Kilometres

9

surprising that the Border Vale villages are more straggling in appearance. Ystradowen, strung out along the ancient roadway from Cowbridge to Llantrisant, is a typical example. Sometimes the churches stand isolated in the fields as at St. Mary Hill and Llanilid, where the only form of settlement is the scattered farmstead. Llansannor and Pendoylan are little more than hamlets of upland type, and are typical of a countryside of forest clearings. But one should not exaggerate the picture. True Norman villages do occur on the more favourable land. Treoes is a perfect example of a street village dating back to the Middle Ages, while Llanharry, Aberthin, Penllyn and Prisk are more like the villages of the Vale. Finally, in a region of many commons, it is more than likely that Trerhingyll, City Llansannor and Craig Penllyn were squatters' villages of fairly recent origin.

The overspill of industry from the coalfield confirms the Border Vale as a transitional zone between Vale and Blaenau, and the nineteenth-century settlements of Pencoed and Llanharan were the result of the exploitation of the South Crop. But mining is not new to the northern fringe of the Border Vale. The Romans came here in search of lead and iron, and Tudor speculators followed in their wake at Llantrisant and Llanharry.

Finally, Pontyclun, a nineteenth-century creation around a railway station, can be viewed in complete contrast to the agricultural and mining villages we have mentioned.

To conclude our introduction to this small but distinct region it is worth mentioning that the Border Vale in the past was as Welsh in speech and outlook as any part of Wales. Almost all the field and farm names are Welsh, and there are no English village names as in the Vale. The common portway or A48 was not the only linguistic divide. About the year 1880, any visitor to the region from Cardiff would be greeted in English at Peterston-super-Ely, but in the local Welsh dialect of the Border Vale in Pendoylan. With the advent of industrialisation and modern transport facilities, the decline in Welsh speaking has been dramatic. In the old Cowbridge Rural District Council area the decline in proportion of Welsh speakers has been from 23.4% in 1901 to 8.1% in 1961. It is interesting to note, however, that the last places to hold out against the tide were the Border Vale villages or Llangan and St. Mary Hill, which had noticeable numbers of bilinguals as late as 1951.

PREHISTORIC TIMES

IN the past writers such as archaeologist Lady Aileen Fox and historian H. J. Randall tended to exaggerate the Border Vale as a barrier to communications between peoples of the coastal plain and the uplands of Glamorgan in prehistoric times. True the dense woodlands, which extended over much of the region, especially on the heavy, impeded soils of the glacial drift, must have been a considerable barrier to movement and colonisation from the beginning. Even today, much of the eastern part of the Border Vale is managed by the Forestry Commission, a striking example of the permanence of geographic controls. Other areas of impenetrable marsh along the Ewenny, Ely and Thaw rivers would have deterred the movement of early man. But it is unreasonable to suggest that primitive man could not get from the Vale to upland Glamorgan, or vice versa, if he wanted to; or settle in the more favourable parts of the Border Vale. Sensitive to the quality of land to a surprising degree, prehistoric man favoured the light, freely drained soils that developed on the open downlands of the area and even on some of the glacial drift itself. It is along these dry routes to the uplands therefore, especially on either side of the River Thaw, that we must look for evidence of the movements of the first peoples.

It is impossible to give an exact date of early man's first penetration of the area. However, there are abundant finds relating to a seasonal occupation of the uplands in Mesolithic (Middle Stone Age) times. It appears that these 'hunters and fishers' lived on the coast in winter, but moved to the uplands following herds of wild cattle and elk in the spring. We know this because they brought beach flints with them as well as using the local chert.

The next phase of human development in South Wales occurred about 5,000 years ago, when the first farmers brought the Neolithic way of life from Western France. These New Stone Age settlers were dark haired, long headed and short in stature. They brought with them a knowledge of pottery as well as agriculture, and they successfully domesticated the dog, horse, sheep, pig and goat. The landscape evidence of the Neolithic culture survives chiefly in the megalithic tombs, huge communal burial places, of which those at Tinkinswood and Maesyfelin in the Vale of Glamorgan are spectacular examples. Their stone implements were more highly polished and had a finer edge, which made it easier to clear the

11

forests, and the various stray finds throughout the Border Vale at Talygarn, Pantwilkin (Welsh St. Donats), Brocastle Farm, and the site of the old Cowbridge Railway Station, seem to indicate that they had accomplished at least a limited clearance of woodland in order to grow barley and corn. There was a surprising degree of human activity, movement and trade within and beyond Wales at this time. The Talygarn axe for example came from Pembrokeshire, and a recently discovered stone adze from Fforest fach, Ystradowen, was derived from the Graig Lwyd 'national' factory at Penmaenmawr.

Early Bronze Age beaker (c. 1800-1600 B.C.), found with a burial at Llanharry

Photograph: National Museum of Wales

The Neolithic culture was followed by the Bronze Age, and about 1800 B.C. there arrived in Glamorgan, probably from across the Bristol Channel, the 'Beaker' Folk, so named from the waisted pots found in their graves. The main concentration of finds lies in the Vale of Glamorgan, especially in the sand dunes of Merthyr Mawr Warren, but there is an important burial within the Border Vale at Llanharry. The site was discovered in September 1929 by some workmen engaged in constructing the line of a new road between Llanharan and Llanharry. They came across a stone cist containing a crouched skeleton and a beaker, lying in a field, known locally as Naboth's Vineyard. The cist was constructed of five sandstone slabs, four uprights and a cover, orientated roughly

Discovery of 'Beaker Find' at Naboth's Vineyard, Llanharry, 1929
Photograph: National Museum of Wales

north and south. Enough of the skeleton was preserved to tell us that the person inside the barrow was a pronounced Beaker man of about five feet nine inches in height, broad headed and probably under thirty-five years of age. He was lying on his right side, with his head facing north, and his knees up to his chin. The pot, which lay alongside the skeleton, is eight inches in height. It is boldly designed and delicately made, similar to other examples found in Somerset. The skeleton, which was cleaned by Mrs. Eliza Johns, an elderly resident of Llanharry, is preserved in the National Museum of Wales.

Of the settlement sites of the Beaker Folk little is known, but it is likely that they were largely nomadic, pastoral people, who practised little or no agriculture. They belong to a transitional period, for although their technology was mainly Neolithic, they had contact with people who had found copper ores in various parts of Western Europe and made a few simple tools. How the Beaker folk reached Llanharry must remain a mystery after 3,500 years, but it is not improbable that they and their fellow pastoralists followed the open countryside along drier routes from Nash Point or thereabouts. Their flocks of sheep and herds of cattle must have roamed in temporary clearings in the moderate forests of beech and oak, which flourished on the lighter soils.

13

With the coming of the Bronze Age, no inroads appear to have been made into the areas of heavy, impeded soils within the Border Vale. The earlier bronze tools occur as chance finds on the lighter soils such as the flat, bronze axe head of simple tooled decoration found recently at Coed y Tranches, near the Ystradown/Llanharry parish boundary on the loamy, well drained Radyr soils on drift. It is quite possibly an import from Ireland about 1500 B.C.

Further Bronze Age finds occur here and there in the Border Vale, but the main concentration of population at the time must have been in the western part of the Vale of Glamorgan. The evidence for this is the remarkable series of cairns and barrows stretching from Nash Point to the famous Golden Mile Barrow in Colwinston. An Early Bronze Age burial has been recorded north of the portway near Llangan School, while a rapier of Middle Bronze Age type has been found near City, Llansannor. This latter find is particularly interesting as the Museum of Wales report for 1905-6 says that other bronze objects were found at this site. If this

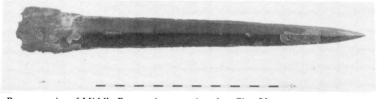

Bronze rapier of Middle Bronze Age type found at City, Llansannor
Photograph: National Museum of Wales

is so it is particularly important because hoards of this date are very rare in South Wales. Other places where Bronze Age people were active are Cowbridge and Coity. A bronze dagger was found with a skeleton in the grounds of Cowbridge Girls' School, while at Coity some charred wheat grains in a deposit at Ponds Cairn of Middle Bronze Age date seem to indicate that there was more reliance on arable farming in the upper portions of the Vale of Glamorgan than has hitherto been realised.

In the late Bronze Age from about 1000 B.C. to 400 B.C. a distinctly local bronze industry appears to have developed in the Cardiff region characterised by the 'South Wales' socketed axe. These axes are well represented by a number of finds in the Border Vale. They have been unearthed at Cowbridge, Fferm Goch (near Llangan), and recently on a housing site on the northern outskirts of Miskin.

The Later Bronze Age and the Early Iron Age (1000-400 B.C.) saw the introduction of iron weapons and implements by a race of people who are thought to have spoken a Celtic language. They made their mark on the landscape of the Vale of Glamorgan in the

Bronze dagger found with a skeleton in the grounds of the Girls' High School, Cowbridge   Photograph: National Museum of Wales

form of hill forts and promontory forts, and their farmsteads, such as the one at Mynydd Bychan near Pentre Meyrick, were well protected with ramparts and ditches. In this warlike and difficult period they built forts in Border Vale country at St. Mary Hill and Llanquian Wood on Stallingdown, yet they avoided the uplands of Glamorgan, where strategic sites were plentiful. Perhaps the settlement sites of Iron Age forts were determined as much by proximity to good grazing and arable land as necessities of defence. The location of the Border Vale forts would enable the Celts to practise a kind of 'transhumance', that is, cultivating the arable lands of the lowlands, while taking advantage of summer grazings of the hill country by moving up their stock.

Of the hill forts themselves little is known. The one at Craig Tan y Lan, St. Mary Hill (SS 958 796) is on closely packed contours and has a single bank and ditch. It seems to be the type of small embanked settlement which is characteristic of South Wales in the Early Iron Age. In Llanquian Wood, near Aberthin, is found a multivallate, Iron Age Camp with wide spaced ramparts. The inner enclosure is oval (140 x 87 m.) with possible entrances to the S.W. and N.W. The outer line of defence ranges from 15 to 40 m. beyond the inner line. It is sited on a slope and is related to the 'hill slope' forts defined by Lady Fox.

15

ROMANS AND CELTIC SAINTS

THE Romans came to South Wales about 75 A.D. Under the leadership of Julius Frontinus, they subdued the Silures of the region and established forts at Caerleon, Cardiff and Neath and possibly one at Cowbridge in the Vale of Glamorgan. When they laid out their famous east-west road the Romans, like the earlier peoples we have mentioned, favoured the freely drained soils of the district, but they must have encountered a major difficulty in crossing the River Thaw. Although it is a mere brook, its valley was a real barrier to communications from east to west. To the north of Cowbridge lay a vast tract of moorland at Penllyn and Llansannor, always liable to flooding, while to the south the valley is narrow and has steep sides. Cowbridge was therefore the only place where a firm road crossing could be established.

From the Antonine Itinerary it is known that a Roman fort called Bomium did exist somewhere in the district. Local historians have been keen to identify this 'Bomium' or 'Bovium' with Cowbridge. More reliable opinion nowadays favours Ewenny as the likely site for the fort, but recent archaeological evidence leaves us in no doubt that a civil settlement of considerable importance grew up at Cowbridge in Roman times.

The settlement lay on either side of the present High Street, with the main concentration of buildings close to the South side and actually underlying the Old Hall. The buildings appear to peter out towards the vicinity of the town wall. The earlier Roman finds at Cowbridge included coins from Trajan to Constantine, including a copper one dedicated to the goddess Roma, some bricks and a bronze fibula. Recently some fragments of flanged roofing tiles, a bone hairpin and numerous shards of samian pottery indicate an important Roman settlement at Cowbridge that lasted from the first to the fourth century A.D.

There is little evidence of Roman colonisation of the Border Vale, however. The Romans preferred to settle in the more favourable land of the Vale. Trallwn (Tre lleng — the township of the legion) in the parish of Llanilid may have been a temporary Roman marching camp like the one at Pen Coed Cae near Beddau. Some coarse Romano-British pottery of the third century has turned up near Llangan School, but the Romanised villa is absent from the district. The Roman villas at Ely and Llantwit Major have been known for many years, but recent discoveries in the Barry area have revealed the existence of additional Roman sites. These villas were the centres of large corn growing estates but were also a hive of industry containing their own smelters for making iron implements such as axes, ploughshares, nails and household utensils. The Romanised Britons, who lived in their luxurious villas, did not have to look beyond the Border Vale for plentiful supplies of raw iron.

The ore occurs in a narrow belt of Carboniferous limestone which extends across the northern part of the Border Vale from Llanharry to Taffs Well. The deposits of iron, often exposed at the surface in rich red tints, had been worked by the natives before the Romans came. A writer in 1859 claimed to have found some old workings at Llechau, near Llanharry, which appeared to be of Roman origin. Some pieces of coarse red pottery said to have been Roman were found at the bottom of an ancient stall workings at Ty Isaf, near Llanharry Recreation Field, while in 1967 a shard from the rim of a Roman cooking pot of the late third century A.D. was dug up in the garden of 'Redlands', again in Llanharry. These pots were apparently the standard cooking jar of the period, and were made at the recently discovered kiln at Caldicot. Traces of an iron industry of Roman origin with smelting done on the spot occur at Miskin, near Llantrisant. A coin of Antonius Pius and some Roman decorated pottery were discovered many years ago under a layer of iron slag in the grounds of Miskin Manor. There is also the possibility that the ore was transported along the ancient roadway from Llantrisant to the Roman fort at Cardiff.

With the departure of the Romans at the end of the fourth century, the history of the Border Vale is veiled in obscurity. Merchants and traders had brought Christianity to South Wales in Roman times. No organised church existed at the time, however. We know that Julius and Aaron, to whom the church of Llanharan is dedicated, were the first Welsh martyrs, dying for their faith at Caerleon in 303 A.D. But it was not until the sixth century that a systematic effort was made to convert the Welsh people to Christianity by the missionary efforts of the Celtic saints. The most important of these were Illtud and Cadoc who set up their monasteries at Llantwit Major and Llancarfan respectively early in the sixth century A.D.

Of the two, St. Illtud and his followers appear to have excited the greater influence in and around the Border Vale, although there is a Cadoc dedication at Pendoylan. It is possible to trace a missionary journey from the Illtud dedications from Llantwit Major, through Llantrithyd, Llanharry, Llantrisant to Llantwit Fardre. Relatives of Illtud, according to tradition, were also active in the locality. The church of Llangan is dedicated to St. Canna, the mother of Crallo, patron saint of Coychurch, and she was the sister-in-law of Illtud himself. St. Canna seems to be further commemorated in Canton, Cardiff (Canna-ton, and Pont-canna).

Other saints connected with the area are St. Sannor (Llansannor) St. Ilid (Llanilid) and St. Owen (Ystradowen), but little or nothing is known about them. It is likely, however, that St. Brynach came to these parts in the wake of the Irish raiders who made constant attacks on the South Wales coast in the fifth century. St. Brynach's church is the isolated, Gothic building in Penllyn parish, now used for occasional services only. According to legend, one of Maelgwyn Gwynedd's men seized one of St. Brynach's cows. A wolf, who was attending the beast, reported the theft to St. Brynach, who was able to retrieve it. Curiously, not far from Llanfrynach is Cowbridge and Llanbleddian ('blaidd' being the Welsh for wolf). Closely associated with the activities of the Celtic saints are the holy wells. One of these is Ffynnon Catwg (St. Cadoc's well near

Celtic Wheel Cross, Llangan

Photograph: Haydn Baynham

Pendoylan church), another is Ffynnon Ceri in Llanilid. Throughout the Middle Ages, wells figured prominently in folk customs and medicinal practices; Llanilid well is one of the few rag wells in Glamorgan. The old custom was to leave the garment of a deceased person in the well, so that the disease which afflicted him would be carried away in the discarded clothes.

One interesting aspect of the missionary activities of the Saints is the actual siting of their churches. Throughout the Border Vale the pre-Norman churches are found almost exclusively on the more favourable land, the exception being Pendoylan, which is sited on the heavy, impeded clays of the glacial drift. In the centuries that followed, the archaeological picture grows faint. However, at Llangan, at least, some remarkable early Christian monuments have survived the ravages of time. One of these is a Celtic Wheel Cross of the tenth or eleventh century. It depicts the Crucifixion in the contemporary Irish manner, itself based upon a Byzantine model. The central figure is Christ, shown as a bearded person, and clad in a long sleeveless tunic. Unlike later representations of the subject, the Saviour's eyes are open and the limbs extended straight along the arms of the cross, instead of being bent. On either side is a soldier piercing the side of Christ with a second soldier bearing a sponge. Another cross of the eleventh century was found lying in fragments in the Rectory garden.

THE NORMANS

WE do not know exactly how and when the Normans conquered Glamorgan. Probably about the year 1093, Robert Fitzhamon launched a sea-borne invasion from Bristol against Iestyn ap Gwrgant, the native ruler of the Kingdom of Morganwg. Having dispossessed Iestyn, Fitzhamon swept through the fertile Vale of Glamorgan south of the portway and divided it into manors among his principal followers. This became the area known as the 'shire fee' of Glamorgan and the knights and their tenants were closely subject to the lord and had to guard his castle at Cardiff for so many days in the year.

The Border Vale, north of the portway, where the three Welsh territories of Talyfan, Ruthin and Miskin (Meisgyn) lay did not yield easily to the Normans. The Welsh put up a strong resistance in this 'wild west' territory, and the conquest was a slow, gradual process and was not finally completed until the later thirteenth century. It is an interesting fact that the boundary of the shire fee runs more or less along the divide between the heavier soils of the Border Vale and the more fertile soils of the coastal plain. The only area where the 'shire fee' extends north of the portway is around Penllyn and Llangan. Here about 1126 Sir Robert le Norris was granted the manor of Penllyn and it was organised on feudal lines with free and unfree tenants working in the open fields. This area of 'shire fee' country is located on some of the more favourable soils north of the portway. Elsewhere in the intermediate tract of country appropriations were made as acts of private enterprise by lords who held their lordship of the Chief Lord, not as knights' fees but as serjeanties. Their power was much greater than that of the knights in the Vale and included power of life and death. It is likely that Talyfan in particular was taken over in a piecemeal fashion by the independent action of a St. Quintin, and Ystradowen Castle mound near the church may have been a temporary structure put up by him in his campaigns against the Welsh. Later to consolidate his victory he built the permanent stone castle at Talyfan a mile away. The siting of Talyfan and Penllyn Castles and the fine motte and bailey castle at Llanilid were clearly part of a scheme of frontier defence against the bulge of Welsh lands, which projected into the Border Vale. They were still ruled over by the sons of Iestyn ap Gwrgant.

The Welsh of Ruthin were particularly troublesome, and it looks as if Samson de Halweia, the owner of the Gelligarn manor of St. Mary Hill, was so harassed with the Welsh raids that he exchanged his knight's fee of Gelligarn for the more comfortable estate of Littleham in Devon, which belonged at the time to Neath Abbey. De Halweia or his predecessor may have built the ring work found at St. Mary Hill (SS 961-787). It is a much eroded site with indications of a bailey to the east side. It is sited within the grange of Gelligarn, so we can assume it was left to ruin by the monks who obviously would not have needed it. I think it likely that in the 'cold war' that developed between the Welsh of the hills and the settled body of the shire, the respective Welsh and Normans were willing to grant some land in the Border Vale around Llanilid and St. Mary Hill to religious bodies whom they respected, thus forming a 'buffer state' between the warring camps.

Ruins of a thirteenth century dovecot at Gelli Garn Grange, St Mary Hill

Photograph: Haydn Baynham

21

The monks of Neath Abbey did not take long to establish a sizeable arable farm at St. Mary Hill. It had 10 carucates, approximately 600 acres under the plough in 1291; a surprisingly large arable farm for the Border Vale even though Gelligarn is situated on the better quality land. The site was explored recently and in the *Report of the Council for Archaeology*, Group 2, 1974, we are told the present day traces of the grange include a large rectangular enclosure defined by a wide spread bank and external ditch. Within this enclosure stands the remains of a thirteenth-century dovecot, now in a sad state of disrepair. Beyond the enclosure considerable evidence of ruined buildings and fragments of medieval dressed stones were discovered. The site may be that of the grange chapel. A strange circular stone-lined pond or cistern was also found nearby.

In the northern part of the Border Vale, especially in the commotes of Ruthin and Miskin, the Welsh chieftains managed to retain a certain degree of control well into the thirteenth century. Ruthin contained Llanharan and Llanilid, while Miskin, like the later Miskin Hundred, extended well into the uplands of Glamorgan. We do not know where the Welsh lords held their courts but tradition has it that the court of the rulers of Miskin was at or near the site of Miskin Manor. R. J. Thomas, an authority on Welsh place names, makes the interesting suggestion that at Pantyquesta near Miskin lived the 'gwestai', who was court provisioner to the Welsh lord. He collected from the freemen of the commote the winter 'gwestfa' of honey, ale, flour and an ox and oats for the lord's horses, and the summer 'gwestfa' of a fat cow, a fat wether and a three-year-old sow. It is only to be expected that such an official should have his seat near the court and significantly Miskin Manor is only one mile away from Pantyquesta.

By the middle of the thirteenth century an opportunity occurred for the Chief Lord, Richard de Clare, to drastically reduce the areas of Welsh autonomy. When Richard Syward, a powerful baron of the member lordship of Talyfan, began to extend his power in the intermediate tract of land between de Clare's demesne in the Vale and the Welsh commotes, a bitter war resulted between him and Howel ap Meredith of Miskin. This gave de Clare the opportunity to act decisively. Syward was accused of levying war and ordered by the county court to keep the truce. He blatantly refused, patched up his quarrel with Howel and they both waged war against Earl Richard. De Clare immediately seized Miskin and using the county court had Syward stripped of his lordships and castle and eventually outlawed. Thus at a stroke, the Chief Lord had acquired not only the Border Vale lordships of Talyfan and Ruthin but the upland commotes of Miskin and Glynrhondda as well. The endemic warfare that characterised the Border Vale was over, and it is significant that it was Richard de Clare who founded the boroughs of Cowbridge and Llantrisant soon afterwards. De Clare also rewarded his own loyal supporters, and he granted the manors of Breigan and Trecastle in the forfeited possessions of Syward to his sheriff Stephen Bauzan and William Scurlage. At Breigan and Trecastle as elsewhere the fortified manor house began to appear on the landscape — a lot later than in the peaceful Vale.

What changes did the Normans bring to their conquered territories in the Border Vale? There is no evidence that they introduced a large population of Anglo Saxon peasants from the West Country as they did in the 'shire fee'. But perhaps a displaced Welsh population moved up and populated the Border Vale as a result. Parts of the conquered lordship of Talyfan were run along the lines of an English manor, but in some of the Border Vale parishes *e.g.* Welsh St. Donats and Pendoylan there may never have been large-scale open fields at all. Some indications of how Talyfan was run may be gleaned from the Inquisition taken 3rd February, 1296, on the death of Gilbert de Clare, son of Richard, who had died in December 1295. We notice that there are 75 free tenants holding 704 acres and 38 customary tenants. This implies only a small degree of communal farming with the rest of the farms widely dispersed throughout the manor, having been carved by enterprising persons out of the waste or forests. The survey does tell us that '53 homesteads of customary tenants are wasted and destroyed by war', so bond villages did exist on the better quality land. The demesne land appears to have been around Talyfan Castle itself and at Maeshwyaid, locally pronounced Masiad. The village of Prisk is not far from here and it is likely to have been a bond village of unfree tenants who cultivated the Lord's demesne. At Llanharry three miles away there was another small corn growing community, but by the time of the Inquisition, it had passed into the hands of the Turbervills of Coity Castle. Apart from the small area of cultivated land, less than a fifth of the total acreage, the rest of Talyfan was densely wooded or wasteland. Four forests are named — Cae Griffith, New Forest, Old Forest and Little Haywood, and there was the Park at Talyfan. Although the population was exclusively Welsh, the manor was run along the lines of an English manor. Most rents were paid not in coins but equivalents; and many holdings were valued at two sparrow hawks a year. Yet in the Border Vale the Normans did not wipe out everything before them as they had done in the shire fee. When Norman lords such as St. Quintin displaced the Welsh lord, he took over his privileges and the Welsh taxes such as the cymorthau were now paid to him

23

instead. Numerous works were rendered to the lord by the customary tenants. They included the carriage of sixty loads of wood for firewood, ploughing, reaping, harrowing, shoeing the ploughing beast and making wheels for wagons and carts, but after the Black Death of 1349-50 there was a great scarcity of labour and these duties were commuted for a money payment. Later documents tell us about the officers who actually administered the lordship. In a Minister's Account mention is made of the Bedell of Talyfan. He was the equivalent of the rhingyll, a minor official of a Welsh commote who collected the rents. Perhaps the little village of Trerhingyll, near Cowbridge, was at that time the administrative centre of the lordship.

The churches of the Border Vale, as we have pointed out, were almost exclusively of Celtic dedication, and it is likely that their

A crusading knight of the time of Agincourt, probably a descendant of Stephen Bauzan. Effigy in the chancel of Llansannor Church

Photograph: Haydn Baynham

pre-Norman structures survived for quite a while after the Conquest until the parishes became rich enough to build larger ones. The Border Vale churches are on the whole small in size and poor in sculptural adornment. Here and there remnants of the medieval churches and their decorations have survived. There is an exceptionally interesting effigy of a cross-legged knight in stone in Llansannor church, which was once thought to be that of Stephen Bauzan, the sheriff of Richard de Clare and the Lord of Breigan. It is of good

24

quality and displays a trend towards naturalism. From the helmet of the reclining knight, we are able to date it to the time of the Battle of Agincourt, or early fifteenth century. It was the fashion in some of the anglicised areas of Glamorgan to raise medieval crosses as an act of piety. It is significant therefore that the churchyards of

Late Norman font at Llanharry Church

Photograph: Haydn Baynham

St. Mary Hill and Llangan are adorned with two fine examples. Fonts of Norman origin have also survived here and there. There are two in the district which are considered more ornate than usual for to quote the *Glamorgan County History*, volume 3, 'those at Llanharry and Llantrisant show either chip-carved diaperwork circular panels or crudely incised leaf sprays'.

25

TUDORS AND STUARTS

THE modern County of Glamorgan, as it existed before local government reorganisation in 1974, came into being as a result of Henry VIII Acts of Union 1536-1543. In modelling it on the contemporary English shire, the Tudors intended that the administration of the new county should devolve upon the leading gentry, who were to hold the offices of sheriff, deputy lieutenant and justice of the peace. Throughout the sixteenth century the leading land-owning families squabbled and quarrelled as they jostled with each other for wealth and position. As the century progressed however, they began to benefit greatly from the strong rule imposed by the Tudors and the long period of peace and economic prosperity that followed.

The dispute over the Border Vale manor of Penllyn which broke out in 1527 illustrates the lawless conditions in Wales on the eve of the Acts of Union. Richard Turbervill had died in 1501 leaving two sons, John and Jenkin. The dispute broke out on the death of John Turbervill when his daughter's claim to the estate was countered by that of Jenkin's son Christopher, who took possession of the manor house. David Jones of Wallington's transcripts of the Star Chamber proceedings tell us what happened next:

'Robert Stradling replied that Christopher: ". . . in most ryotous and forcyble manner accompanied by dyvers ryotous and mysruled persons had entered the said dwelling house . . .", the rumour of which having passed around, an assembly of friends and kinsmen of both parties made for Penllyn, where upon Robert Stradling went, so he claims, to preserve the King's peace and called upon the rioters to depart in the King's name: ". . . at whych time the said Christopher with the number of XXV ryotous persons or thereabouts with hym within the said house kepying of the same with force, that is to say with long bowes, arrowes, billes and other weapons".'

The dispute was finally resolved by arbitration and Christopher kept the manor of Penllyn.

Turbulent and hot-headed as the gentry were, they accepted in the main the great changes brought about by the Reformation. The dissolution of the monasteries in particular enabled certain of the land-hungry gentry to acquire new wealth within the Border Vale. As the land of Neath Abbey at Gelligarn and the dissolved Order of

St. John came on to the market, it was quickly bought up by Sir Rice Mansel of Margam and John Bassett of Bonvilston respectively. Yet when the Elizabethan church settlement was imposed on the people in 1559, there does seem to have been some determined opposition to it from within the Border Vale and elsewhere in the county. William Dawkins of Llansannor and Thomas Williams of Llanharry almost certainly left their rectories to protest against the Elizabethan settlement. The most prominent among Glamorgan recusants were, however, the Turbervill family who bravely protected the old faith at Penllyn. Morgan Clynnog, a missionary priest in Wales, was living secretly with Jenkyn Turbervill in Penllyn Castle in 1596 when the house was searched. Many severe laws were passed against the recusants between 1571 and 1611, and they were forced to pay as much as £20 a month for non-attendance at Church. Despite these humiliations, the Turvbervill family remained steadfast to Roman Catholicism for over two hundred years. In 1678 the priest John Lloyd was arrested at Penllyn Castle, while serving the Turbervill family, and committed for trial as a suspected popish priest or Jesuit. Found guilty he was hanged, drawn and quartered on the Little Heath outside Cardiff on 22nd July 1679. The same day Father Phillip Evans, a Catholic priest who had been arrested at Sker, the house of another branch of the Turbervills, suffered the same fate. Fathers Lloyd and Evans were beatified by

Llansannor Court, historic home of the Gwyn family   Photograph: Haydn Baynham

Pope Pius XI in 1929, and were canonised by Pope Paul VI on 25th October 1970.

Although much of the property of the Border Vale was beginning to pass into the hands of powerful absentee owners such as the Earls of Pembroke and the Sidneys, at a rather lower social level a numerous class of squires was coming to the fore. Chief among these were the Gwyns of Llansannor, the Williams of Aberthin, and the Jenkins of Hensol. How the Gwyns of Llansannor succeeded while their cousins the Thomases of Breigan declined in social status is a mystery. By advantageous purchase and marriages they began to build up their property. Adding to the core of their estate around Llansannor Court they began to buy up the freehold and copyhold land within the parish and acquire land in most of the surrounding parishes. Like other Welsh gentry families, the Gwyns managed to secure rich brides in successive generations. The marriage of Richard ap Howel Thomas of Llansannor to the daughter and co-heiress of Griffith Ychan of Ystradyfodwg secured several farms in the Rhondda valley in a rich pastoral region, noted for its cattle and sheep rearing. In the middle of the sixteenth century, John Gwyn married Jane, sister of Sir Rice Mansel of Margam, but the most propitious match of all was that between Edward Gwyn of Llansannor Court and Eleanor, daughter of Sir Francis Popham of Littlecote in Wiltshire, since it brought the family into a close and profitable relationship with the English Court, and some of the richest families, providing connections and the patronage that accompanied them.

Several of the squires' houses of this period still survive. They are small and unpretentious, yet mansions such as Llansannor

Great House, Aberthin   Photograph: Haydn Baynham

Court and Great House, Aberthin, have about them a singular charm and distinction. Llansannor Court probably dates from the late sixteenth century. The beautiful arch doors and graceful mullioned windows give ample evidence of this. Massive oak beams support the ceiling and between each beam the decorative plaster shows signs of primitive finger plastering. Some beautiful original oak panelling with a decorative frieze of birds still exists.

Great House, Aberthin, situated in a picturesque valley that skirts the northern extremity of Stallingdown, is a delightful manor house with high gables, which was probably built in the second quarter of the seventeenth century. It has a fine symetrical south front and was formerly roofed with stone slabs. It has a charming little gatehouse entered by a bridge over the Aberthin brook. An earlier arch was probably reused for its outer doorway. The original sun-dial over the porch bore the date 1658 and the initials 'R.W.' which stands for Robert Williams, the owner of the house at that time. The Williams family, who were distant cousins of the Gwyns of Llansannor, were of considerable standing in the locality in the early seventeenth century. Robert Williams' father, William ap Thomas of Aberthin, probably built the house, but the family soon died out and it eventually became part of the Dynevor estate.

Like most of the important land-owners of the county, the gentry of the Border Vale favoured the King in his struggle with Parliament. One Border Vale squire, Judge Jenkins of Hensol, was so

David Jenkins of Hensol

Photograph: National Portrait Gallery

formidable a champion of the King's cause that he declared himself quite willing to die on the scaffold with the Bible under one arm and the Magna Carta under the other. Upon being arraigned at the Bar of the House of Commons the redoubtable Judge refused to kneel in respect and was fined one thousand pounds for contempt. After narrowly escaping the scaffold on several occasions he was pardoned and set free in 1656.

With the defeat of King Charles I in 1645, it did not take Parliament long to launch its grand project of converting the people of Wales to puritanism. The Propagation Act of 1650 set up a Commission whose aims were to destroy the old established system and replace it by a new order. The first task was to eject the Anglican clergy and over 278 clergymen were removed from their livings within the first three years of the Act. In the Border Vale, almost all the clergymen were turned out for a variety of reasons and a few suffered real privation. One of the most unfortunate cases was that of Edmond Gamage, the Rector of Llanharry. John Walker gives the following description of him: 'He was Turn'd out some time before the Year 1649; and not only Dispossest of his House, Glebe & but the very Tythe-Corn, that he had brought in some Weeks before, was Seiz'd upon; and not a grain of it, or any Fifths allowed him towards the Subsistence of his Large Family; So that he was forc'd to Quit the Place, and Retire to a small Pittance of his own, until the Restoration. Upon which he Returned to his Living; but Enjoyed it a very little while. One Howel Thomas, and one Thomas Joseph, both Anabaptists, Occasionally held forth in his Church, during the Usurpation'. Other clergymen were more

Sir Leoline Jenkins

Photograph: National Portrait Gallery

fortunate: Francis Davies of Llangan, for example, provided for himself by keeping a school.

No account of the seventeenth century would be complete without mention of Sir Leoline Jenkins the distinguished lawyer, diplomat and pioneer in education of the Restoration period. He was born at Maendy (some say Talygarn) in 1623. He was educated at Jesus College, Oxford, but his studies were interrupted by the Civil War. After many adventures, he was forced to flee abroad because of his royalist sympathies. While abroad he acquired a deep knowledge of Civil Law which was to greatly advance his public career later on. After the Restoration he became Principal of Jesus College, Oxford, and in 1665 he was appointed to preside over the High Court of Admiralty. His work as Judge in that Court is said to have been of prime importance in the history of Prize Law. As a diplomat he won some success also and represented England at the famous Congress of Nymegen. In 1680 he was appointed Secretary of State and led the Court Party against the Exclusion Bill. He also played an important part in the discovery of the Rye Plot to murder Charles II. As a servant of the Crown, Jenkins was conscientious and honest. Pepys, the diarist, wrote of him: 'I am mightily pleased with the Judge, who seems a very rational, learned and uncorrupt man'. He has been described as the second founder of Jesus College having placed it on its feet after the Restoration, and he was a benefactor of Cowbridge Grammar School. He died in 1685.

EARLY MODERN TIMES 1700-1850

THE eighteenth century was the period when the landed gentry rose to the zenith of their power and influence. Over the previous two centuries they had been steadily building up their estates, and by the this time the land, and the social and political power that went with it, became concentrated in a few hands. In the sixteenth century the small free-holders were still common in Border Vale parishes like Pendoylan, but by the eighteenth century their properties had been swallowed up by the large estates of the Aubreys of Llantrithyd and the Jenkins of Hensol. Now over half the land belonged to no more than a dozen or so major landowners, with the Marquess of Bute, the Gwyns of Forde Abbey, the Aubreys of Llantrithyd and the Earls of Leicester well to the fore. There was a remarkable pocket of resistance to this trend, however, at Treoes near Llangan. Here there were a large number of yeoman farmers still cultivating the strips in the open fields in the medieval fashion and they were to continue to do so well into the nineteenth century. No one landowner had been able to control the destinies of these redoubtable yeomen of Treoes who in face of the economic pressure of the times had tenaciously hung on to their small fragmented properties scattered in a haphazard fashion in the open fields. The story is the more remarkable when one realises that in the neighbouring parish of St. Mary Hill the Aubreys of Llantrithyd had successfully managed to control the whole of the land of the parish.

The manner in which the eighteenth-century squires built up their estates often included unscrupulous practice of the law and sometimes downright dishonesty. The rise of the Powell family of Llanharan, one of the old Welsh uchelwyr families from the Maesteg region, is a typical story of eighteenth-century skulduggery and vile corruption. From the notebooks of David Jones of Wallington the details of the charges against Rees Powell, Squire of Llanharan, are set out in the records of the Court of Chancery. It appears that one Morgan Powell, a native of Llangynwyd, had emigrated to Jamaica early in the eighteenth century and amassed a fortune of £40,000. He died without issue and the estate should have been divided among his eight brothers and sisters. Although proclamations were issued in all the market towns of Glamorgan concerning the money, it seems that Rees Powell of Llanharan got

32

Llanharan House Photograph: Haydn Baynham

to hear of the circumstances, and knowing that the brothers and sisters were illiterate and were living in an isolated place, took advantage of them and obtained at least £20,000 of the money simply by pretending that he was the next of kin to the deceased Morgan Powell. Some of the relatives when they heard of their rights appealed to Sir Humphrey Mackworth, the Neath industrialist, to look into the matter. But Rees Powell sent his wife Elizabeth to intercept Sir Humphrey on the Golden Mile and bribe him with a sum of £1,500 not to impart to the relatives any of the information he had discovered about the fortune. Sir

Argoed Ganol Photograph: Haydn Baynham

Hensol Castle

Photograph: Haydn Baynham

Penllyn Castle

Photograph: Haydn Baynham

Humphrey promptly pocketed the money and Rees Powell was able to use his illegally acquired fortune to build Llanharan House in 1757 — a rather severe three-storey dwelling set at the foot of the Garth Maelwg. It is now the home of George Williams, the well-known industrialist.

In certain parishes of the Border Vale there is some evidence of neglect by absentee landlords. At Llansannor, for instance, the Court, Breigan House and several of the old farmsteads were in a sorry state of dilapidation throughout much of the eighteenth century. Argoed Ganol surprisingly appears to have been the principal house in Llansannor after 1750 and a rich property owner called Edward Thomas lived there. Elsewhere the picture that emerges is of a prosperous landed interest, and several of the ancient seats of the district were extended or rebuilt during the period. In 1735 Hensol Castle was extended by Lord Talbot, who added two wings and two square battlemented towers, while Miss Emilia Gwinnett rebuilt Penllyn Castle towards the end of the century on the exact spot where Sargent Seys' house had previously stood in ruins.

The Napoleonic Wars brought great prosperity to the region and the resulting inflation made marginal heathland profitable to cultivate. When Sir John Aubrey encroached upon the New Forest near Ystradowen his rights were hotly disputed by John Fraunceis Gwyn of Forde Abbey. After a famous quarrel they decided to partition the common between them. With the advent of the Industrial Revolution came a new kind of landowner on the scene as the newly-rich capitalists eagerly sought to buy up country estates and enjoy the social privileges that went with them. As fortunes were made in South Wales itself the ironmasters, in particular, began to buy up land; it was an ironmaster, William Crawshay, who in 1835 commissioned the remarkable mock-gothic castle of Hensol from J. H. Wyatt, one of the leading architects of his day.

Much has been written about the decline in religion in Glamorgan prior to the Methodist Revival. Throughout most of the Border Vale parishes, the chief abuses of poverty, pluralism and non-residence were present throughout the eighteenth century. At Llansannor in 1718, for instance, the incumbent was a Mr. Cooke, about whom the following comments were made in a church document of the time: 'The present incumbent is Mr. Wm. Cooke, who seldom troubles these cures (Newcastle, Tythegston and Bettws) for he hath two other Churches at some distance to look after. How he came to huddle up so many Churches is not my business to inquire, but this I am assur'd. He is as poor as a Church mouse'.

However, with the conversion of Daniel Rowland and Howel

Harris in 1735 the revitalising influences of Methodism was soon to spread throughout the Border Vale and awaken the church from its slumber. Of the great Methodist preachers to visit the district the most powerful and influential was Howel Harris (1714-1773). Harris came to Mid-Glamorgan in 1739 and visited Hopkin Rees at St. Mary Hill Court, where he was most cordially welcomed. His next call was at Collenau in Tonyrefail, the home of the Pritchard family, which was to become such a strong pillar of Methodism in that part of Glamorgan. On that particular day he rode over to Llanharry to attend morning service in the parish church. Whenever Howel Harris and the other great revivalists preached, the converts were grouped together into 'seiadau' or societies. These 'seiadau' at first regarded themselves as reforming agencies within the Church, but as they grew they built for themselves meeting places and eventually developed into the body now known as the Presbyterian Church of Wales. By 1743, mainly as a result of Howel Harris' preaching, three 'seiadau' had been established within the Border Vale at Llanharry, Aberthin and Llanilid. A year later the revival had gained a firm footing at Mynydd Ruthin, where to quote Thomas William, Eglwys Ilan 'is a great congregation come to hear and a few Lambs of the Lord Jesus beginning to Assemble themselves together'.

By 1768 there seems to have been a distinct falling away from the faith within the area mainly because of the rift between the two great leaders Howel Harris and Daniel Rowland. Fortunately the flame was kept alive in a small society that had been formed in Ton Breigan cottage, Llansannor. At that critical moment David Jones was presented to the living of Llangan and under his remarkable ministry, the little church of Llangan became the rendezvous of huge crowds of people in search of knowledge and spiritual guidance. They came from as far afield as Margam, Pyle, Llangynwyd, Neath, Coychurch and Cardiff, and made Llangan as well known as Llangeitho in Cardiganshire. A new chapter was being written in the history of Methodism and by the end of the Napoleonic Wars the tide had swung decisively in favour of nonconformity with chapels springing up in most of the villages of the area.

FARMS, FAIRS AND COUNTRY CUSTOMS

THROUGHOUT most of the nineteenth century the majority of people derived their livelihood from agriculture. There was, it is true, some small scale mining at Llanharry and Llangan for much of the period, but the overspill of industry from the coal field did not really occur until the third quarter of the century, and only then did the townships of Pontyclun, Llanharan and Pencoed spring up along the line of the South Wales railway. Farms in the Border Vale were, on the whole, smaller than those of the Vale and there has always been a greater concentration on pastoral than arable farming. However, a hundred years or so ago, a great deal more emphasis was placed on the growing of corn than there is today. On nearly every farm, wheat was produced for flour, barley for the malt house, and oats for the animals. With the large scale importation of cheap corn and the growth of industry immediately to the north of the region, the farmers of the Border Vale were forced to turn their attention to the production of milk. Except during wartime, the trend away from arable farming has never been reversed. Agriculture in the region today is still based on

Ystradowen, Pendoylan and District Sheep Shearing Society, 1930

dairying, although summer fattening of cattle is also practised. Sheep are found on nearly all farms and there are a few specialist pig producers. Friesian herds usually average about thirty cows and only in the last few years has the yard and parlour system of milking replaced the old-fashioned cowsheds. Most of the farms of the Border Vale are less than a hundred acres and are run by small family businesses.

To return to the Border Vale of the middle years of the nineteenth century, David Jones of Wallington wrote that all those who had farming stock of produce to sell, or who were requiring to buy household necessities, came to Cowbridge on Market Days. The farmer would always ride on his carthorse with his wife seated behind him carrying a large basket full of butter, cheese, eggs and poultry. As they journeyed through each village, they were often passed by the pack mules, which at that time conveyed thousands of tons of coal from Llanharry Meadow to Cowbridge and most of the villages of the Vale. Men and occasionally women such as Sallie Mulsod would be in charge of twelve or more mules at a time. At Cowbridge market every conceivable article from a tallow candle to a scythe or rake could be purchased. One commodity which was in short supply, however, was fresh meat. Most ordinary families could afford only one meal of pork or mutton for their Sunday dinner. Beef was a luxury and the gentry alone could afford to buy it. The life of the farm labourer was very hard, but in the early years of the last century his wages were higher than in most parts of the country, and in 1850 he could expect to earn about twelve shillings a week. Their cottages were small, and sometimes, like Rock Cottage, St. Mary Hill, quite picturesque. Often the cottagers squatted on the common land as at City, Llansannor. Usually they were clean and tidy, but there were exceptions, as E. M. Miles tells

Rock Cottage, St Mary Hill, a typical labourer's smallholding

us in his 'Reminiscences of Cowbridge and District' published in the *Glamorgan Gazette* in the 1930's: 'I remember going to Penylan when a boy and visiting a small cottage occupied by an old woman, whose name I withhold. The front and only door opened into her room on the ground floor where there was a bedstead with a bed and a heap of rags thereon. Fowls were walking about the room and a pig seemed to be treated as one of the family. The floor under the bed was stored with swedes or field turnips which gave a very pungent aroma to the room'. Writing in 1879, Daniel Owen of Ash Hall, Ystradowen, could justly feel proud that the Glamorgan farmers were well in advance of their neighbours across the Bristol Channel in procuring agricultural implements. He tells us that McCormick's combined reaper and self binder had been tried out early on the Border farm of Llwynhelig, near Cowbridge, in the presence of many well-known agriculturalists of the county. He recalled the time when as a boy he would go to a reaping harvest with as much gusto as attending St. Mary Hill Fair. At that time a farmer wishing to cut ten acres of wheat would employ thirty or forty reapers with their sickles. Women and boys would attend to the binding, but it was considered rather degrading for a man to bind. The wages were higher at reaping time than at the rest of the year; the harvesters would receive two shillings a day and their food, while the binders would be given one shilling and their food. In time the sickle was replaced by the scythe, which cost the farmer a mere seven shillings an acre to cut his fields compared with thirteen shillings an acre using the sickle.

The red letter day in every farmer's calendar was 26th August, the date of St. Mary Hill Fair. It was not only patronised by the farmers and horse traders but by the local tradesmen as well, for the fair in its heyday was one of the best places in Glamorgan to

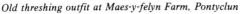

Old threshing outfit at Maes-y-felyn Farm, Pontyclun

seek a bargain or make a sale. The history of the fair goes back to Medieval times when it was held on 15th August on the feast of the Assumption of the Virgin Mary. In Elizabethan times the Fair was regarded as one of the most dangerous places in Glamorgan, and its reputation for lurid happenings never entirely left it. A popular belief has always been that rain was regularly sent on 26th August to wash the blood away. In earlier times the old Welsh drovers of the hill country would move their large herds of livestock from St. Mary Hill across the Brecon Beacons to Hereford and other English markets, and the coming of the railways in the 1850's made the fair one of the most famous horse fairs in Britain. The

Hay-making at Hendrewen, Llanharan, about 1920

Fair also attracted thousands of people who went simply to enjoy themselves. The fairground was crammed with amusements which catered for all sorts of tastes, including swinging boats, fat and thin lady shows, wild animals, boxing booths, flea shows and fortune tellers galore. It was the occasion of the year on which to meet old friends from afar. No one missed attending if he could help, and people like David Reynold of Penllyn claimed to have attended seventy-five fairs in succession. In the evening the fairground became a veritable battleground as men and youths from rival parishes fought each other until darkness fell.

In any agricultural community there will be found customs of ancient origin whose themes are the age-old dramas of death,

40

birth, and fertility. An unusual funeral custom was practised at Llansannor in the early years of this century when four little girls were invited to be bearers at a baby girl's funeral and accompany the coffin from the City cottages to Llansannor Church. At the end of the service each girl was presented with a pair of white gloves by the bereaved parents to symbolise the continuation of life in the little ones who were left. Many of the old customs were associated with the harvest and can probably be traced back to Roman times or earlier. During the corn harvest there was always a good deal of larking going on among the reapers. After taking luncheon on the field, a young man would take hold of a young girl, throw her on to the ground and attempt to kiss her. If he succeeded he was considered to be a man, but if he failed he would be looked upon as a duffer.

An amusing custom practised by the local farmers was that of taking their dogs to church or chapel on Sundays. The dogs, suitably attired, one guesses, in their Sunday best collars, would normally sit quietly by their master's side throughout the service. If the sermon dragged on the local farmers had the remedy. They would unleash their canine companions and the resulting scuffling, snarling and barking would not only drown the droning from the pulpit, but would bring one of the deacons armed with a special elongated pair of tongs called a gefel to oust the offending hounds from the house of God. Not all the dogs, it seems, had a bad name. An elderly resident of Penllyn has informed me that 'Carlo' of Moorland's Farm, Penllyn, was exceptionally well behaved on the Lord's Day in the last century. When illness or the harvest kept the family away from chapel, the faithful old dog would trot along, seek out the family seat, and sit reverently throughout the service.

The final meet of the Glamorgan Hunt in the northern part of the Border Vale, January 1976   Photograph: Haydn Baynham

Fox hunting has always been a popular pastime in the Border Vale since the first hunt was established by Squire Richard Hoare Jenkins of Llanharan House about the year 1805. The old Squire with his faithful huntsman Shoni Harry hunted the Trecastle Woods, Coed-y-Fforest, Talygarn, and the Garth Maelwg for over half a century. About 1873 the Glamorgan Hunt was started by Theodore Mansel Talbot, son of C. R. M. Talbot of Margam. He established hunt kennels and stables at Llandough, near Cowbridge. In the previous year he had obtained permission to hunt the whole of the county south of the main railway line from Cardiff to Bridgend. The only snag was the shortage of foxes, the animal having become almost extinct in the area. So a number of French foxes had to be procured before hunting could begin. One family closely connected with the Glamorgan Hunt has been the Homfrays of Penllyn Castle: J. R. Homfray was master of the Cowbridge hounds about 1870; H. R. Homfray was master fo the Glamorgan Hunt and the late Captain Homfray was master in the 1950s and was always known locally as 'The Master'.

INDUSTRY

APART from the mining of lead at Mwynd, near Llantrisant, in the Middle Ages, there is little evidence that the rich deposits of iron, lead and coal were worked to any great extent until the more settled times of the Tudors. But the greater opportunity offered by the Act of Union for English capital to be utilised in extracting the ores meant the beginnings of industry in the locality. As early as 1531 a speculator named John Ellis was commissioned to search for iron and lead ores in the Royal Park near Llantrisant and about thirty men were employed in clearing a site at a wage of 6d a day. At about the same time the St. Thomas, St. John and St. Peter mines were started at Mwyndy nearby. Leland, the antiquary to Henry VIII, also mentioned these early mines in the neighbourhood of Pontyclun. He wrote: 'There were two fair Parkes by South of Lantrissent now onpalid and without Deere. There is now Yren made in one of these Parkes named Glinog'.

Further west the iron resources of the Llanharry district were soon to be exploited by the well-known Sussex ironmasters, the Sidneys. They had been forced to look elsewhere for new fields of operation for their charcoal furnaces by an Act of Elizabeth I forbidding the felling of timber in the south of England. Fortunately, through his marriage in 1584 to the heiress of Coity, the ironmaster Robert Sidney came into possession of the Llanharry manor with its abundance of woodland and pockets of high grade ore. The mines at Llanharry and Mwyndy were very small and dangerous. One consisted of a shaft about 30 feet deep and only three men worked in it, one hewing, one timbering and the third extracting the ore. An extensive trade was established by the English ironmasters and there are records of iron being shipped to Gloucester, Bristol, Rye and even Dublin. However, after about 1600 the iron trade decreased rapidly, mainly because of the development of iron fields outside the county.

Lead mining is not usually associated with this part of the county, but when Walter Davies visited Glamorgan about 1815 he found several mines in operation in the Border Vale. The most important were at Tewgoed near Llangan and the Park mine near Llantrisant. Mining at Llangan and Llantrisant had been active throughout the seventeenth and eighteenth centuries, when large

Stack of nineteenth-century lead mine near Gelliaraul, Llangan

Photograph: Haydn Baynham

quantities of lead were exported from the port of Aberthaw. The ore was also smelted on the spot at Llangan about the middle of the eighteenth century and during its passage through Cowbridge it was liable to be taxed. According to Walter Davies over 500 miners were employed in the Park mine near Pontyclun in the eighteenth century and from 1757 to 1760 over 402 tons were extracted from this particular mine. The next phase in the history of lead mining was the middle years of the nineteenth century when companies were formed to run the Tewgoed and Gelliaraul mines at Llangan. At this latter site today stands the ruins of an engine house and the boiler house stack, about twenty feet high. These mines were successful for a while and a *Glamorgan Gazette* journalist tells us that the lead miners were the 'aristocrats of the sons of toil' in the district. The *Fox and Hounds* inn at Penllyn did a roaring trade patronised by lead miners from Cornwall earning the remarkably high wages of 24 shillings a week.

The earliest coal pits in operation in the Border Vale date to the beginning of the seventeenth century when in 1602 Sir Robert Sidney and his wife Lady Barbara leased their coal pit on Llanharry meadow to Edward Davie at a yearly rent of 10 shillings. By 1775 there was a flourishing colliery on the same common and during the last century the pit near Torgelly farm supplied the needs of Cowbridge and most of the Vale. By 1817, the Trecastle Coal Works was also in full operation and prospects for mining appeared

South Rhondda Colliery, Llanharan, 1912

so bright that plans were made to construct a tramway from Trecastle to Cowbridge. The future of coalmining, however, lay with Pencoed and Llanharan where deep pits were sunk into the south crop after 1850 at Cribbwr Main, Raglan, Glamorgan South, South Rhondda and Meiros.

At Pontyclun and Llanharry, however, there was a dramatic growth in the production of iron-ore in the second half of the nineteenth century. West of the River Ely were the Bute and Mwyndy mines, which were extensively worked in the period after 1854. These mines brought in workers from Cornwall, whose descendants still live in the little village of Brynsadler nearby. West of the Ely river, there was a flourishing concern at the 'Patch', Llanharry, in the 1860's, while the Trecastle mine produced over 120,000 tons of ore, all from one large pocket. This particular pit was forced to close down in 1891 mainly because of competition from Spanish ores. No further iron was raised in the parish until the Llanharry Haematite iron-ore mine was opened in 1901. For many years it was the only iron-ore mine working in Wales. Until its closure on 25th January 1976 some 200,000 tons were railed annually from Llanharry to Guest Keen Iron and Steel Works at East Moors, Cardiff, where it was used to produce high quality pig iron for castings. In recent years the Mine Ambulance Team brought

First aid champions at Llanharry mine. Mr D. B. Ryan displays the F.D.S. Hollings Cup

much credit to management and men. Captained by David B. Ryan, the team carried off the valuable F. D. S. Hollings Cup on seven occasions. In 1971 the team qualified to compete in the National Finals at Warrington. The present team consists of D. B. Ryan, T. D. Downes, T. Harwood, N. Fantini and E. Wooding. The closure of the Llanharry mine was a sad blow to all those associated with it. To mark the occasion an article on the mine was written for the *Llantrisant Observer* by one of the longest-serving miners, Councillor Harry Lewis. By kind permission of the editor of that newspaper, we are reproducing most of this article, which we feel will be of great interest to readers:

'The closing down of Llanharry Iron Ore Mine today (Friday, 25th July) brings to an end not only seventy-four years production of iron-ore, but it sadly closes a chapter of close and constant association in the lives of its present complement of 240 men, the majority of whom have become entwined with the mine for the greater part of their lives. Men like Howard Dingle, one of the winding enginemen, whose father the late William Dingle was a winding engineman before him, and whose grandfather Cornishman (Cap'n) William Dingle, helped in cutting the first sod and became the first manager when the mine opened in 1901 after an abortive attempt by another company to sink a shaft several years earlier.

Foremost among long serving workers at the mine were Fred

Cutting the first sod at Llanharry iron-ore mine, 1901

Photograph: Jack Williams

Medley, the blacksmith with fifty-two years service, Johny Davies, the lamproom attendant and former miner (44 years), Bill Owen, chief electrician (43 years), Bill Dean, former ostler and latterly bath-house attendant, and scores of miners like Fred Newble, Edgar Rosser, Noel Wardle, Will John, John David, Cecil Taylor, Harold Ashcroft, the brothers Fred and Jack Monks, Phil Williams, Stan Price, Alf Davies, Ted Trebble, Bill Ambury (the first 'boy' to be employed underground), Henry Painter, Ernie Deakin and Harry Howell.

No one can easily forget the characters, past and present, like the Harbour Lights, Dai Byatts, Jim Cabbage, Applejack, Josh Rowe, Big Bill Burrows, Slogger Powell, China Birch, Tommy Trouble and Wally the Welsh Pole. These characters started work when Glamorgan Haematite Iron-Ore Company flourished as a private concern under the managing directorship of the late Stuart Martin of Pantyquesta who employed 500 men in the only iron-ore mine in Wales, which produced in its heyday 200,000 tons of high grade hematite-ore per annum.

In the earlier years, 22 pit ponies were used in the transportation of the ore from the working places to the bottom of the 520 feet shaft. Haulage engines and electric locos took over later, and in May 1963, stable companions like Cymro, who loved to drink from the miners' tea bottles, Star, King, Windsor and the devious Duke, who could count the clink of the tightening shackles and would refuse to proceed if more than the requisite number were hitched up behind him, were pensioned-off on to pastures green.

Tipping waste material on the surface of Llanharry iron-ore mine

Every miner wore clogs in the early days and green tallow candles provided illumination underground. Then came carbide lamps, and finally electric cap lamps. The ore miner knows hard work and danger. Iron rock doesn't land lightly from above, neither is it light to lift on the shovel. It is mighty hard to bore and blast, and the fact that water follows everywhere makes working conditions both wet and cold. The amount of water contained in the mine can be gauged from the fact that several powerful electric turbines between them pumped on average almost 100 million gallons annually to the surface, to make electricity charges one of the highest overheads and one of the biggest headaches for the management when power cuts prevailed.

Presentation of long service awards at Llanharry iron-ore mine

Despite the hazards however, the Haematite was a happy mine and one the men and management will miss very much. As one manager, the late D. Welsh, put it during a long-service presentation ceremony in the '60's: 'Ours is a mine without malice.'

Possibly no other mine in the country has had fewer disputes than the one that put Llanharry on the map — just a few weeks' strike action spread over three-quarters of a century! Apart from a few prickles of pay disputes — quite a regular feature everywhere these days — a happy, easy-going relationship has reigned between management and men throughout the life of the mine. Few employees have been in a hurry to leave and seek employment elsewhere. This is proved by the fact that sixty per cent of the men have earned long-service awards and quite a number have retired after half a century of service.

The peak period of production was enjoyed at the mine immediately prior to and during the Second Word War. In 1948, owing to an acute shortage of local labour, a large number of Poles came over to work in the mine, and several years later Italian labour was imported.

They found it difficult at first — trying to sort out what was what and what was wanted — in sign language, but through the infinite patience and understanding of their mine 'butties' coupled with their own willingness to work, they soon became an asset to production and international relationship.

Mel Thomas, the present manager, may have a brusque manner, but deep down everyone acknowledges that he is 'not a bad old stick'. A former colliery official, he has completed fifty years of underground work — half of it at the Llanharry mine.

Under-manager Cliff O'Neill was formerly 'on the iron' for many years and is also a past Chairman of the NUM Lodge. He too is highly regarded by the men, as are shift bosses John Watkins, Chairman of Glamorgan Rugby Club, Frank Wareham, Brian Groves, Pat Griffin, Keith Parsons, Ken Reeves and Keith John — all a grand bunch of bosses, not forgetting Edgar Maggs, the mine agent, a comparative newcomer but nevertheless one of a grand team.

And so, a mine dies and is mourned by many who will miss it sorely, much as one does when one says farewell to a family. The giant pit-head wheels will no longer revolve to raise the rust-coloured rock or the red-hued miners to the surface sunshine, and 1,000 feet below the galleyways and caverns will cease to echo to the rattle of trams, locos, Emcos and boring machines.

'On top' the banter in the bath-house dies down and a strange silence prevails where once there was ceaseless chatter and chaffing in the changing rooms. Millie (Mrs. Hopkins) is stopping shop in the canteen and, perhaps most important of all, cashiers Haydn Morris and Lloyd Hughes will never again push that precious pay packet through the pigeonhole.

What then is left? A couple of conical, copper coloured tips, a silent shaft — and the water. Water from its source beyond the Black Mountains, which will swirl around the workings to set a seal on a mine that has overtaken life's span of three score years and ten'.

The construction of the South Wales railway in 1850 attracted the Victorian industrialists to Pencoed and Pontyclun. At Pencoed

Female and juvenile workers at the Pontyclun Tin Works, c. 1904

a foundry and a brickworks were established, while at Pontyclun were located a Pipe and Sanitary Works and the Ely Tin Plate works. The former which started as Messrs. Noel Ltd. was one of the largest of its kind in Wales, covering several acres. By 1898, the company had built up a large export business with orders from Europe and South America. Later the Pipe Works used to concentrate on manufacturing drainpipes, chimney pots and earthenware utensils. The Tin Plate Works in 1898 was the property of W. H. Edwards and was capable of turning out 20,000 boxes per week and employed 300 hands. On our photograph are some of the female and juvenile labourers of about 1904. The hours of work were from 6.30 a.m. to 5.30 p.m. The female workers got 8/- per week and Mrs. Cassie Dodd of Pontyclun is one of the few surviving members.

In the post-war years new industry has come to various sites in the Llantrisant areas to offset the decline of the coal-mining industry which had operated along the southern outcrop of the coalfield. There were plans for considerable development of the remaining reserves of coal, and several million pounds was invested in Llanharan colliery only to see it close down soon afterwards. Of the new manufacturing industries that have been established at Talbot Green, Pontyclun and Llanharan in the last few years, space allows a brief treatment of one or two concerns. The Royal Sovereign Pencil Company is an example of a London-based firm

51

Pipe Works, Pontyclun

moving its manufacturing unit to Pontyclun in 1946 in line with the government policy of the time. Expansion took place in 1962 with the absorption of another London-based pencil making company — Pencils Ltd., of Tottenham. Four years later the name 'Royal Sovereign Staedtler Limited' was adopted to signify joint ownership by W. Patterson and Company of Beckenham and J. S. Staedtler of Nurnberg. The origins of J. S. Staedtler date back to 1782 and Nurnberg has always been the home of pencil-making in Germany. In 1973 the present title of the firm, Staedtler (U.K.) Limited, was adopted to signify the association with numerous other Staedtler companies throughout the world in Australia, Brazil, Malaysia, Spain and South Africa.

The small firm too has an important role to play to ensure a continuing industrial expansion in the locality. P. Gwyn Humphrey and Son (Engineers) Ltd. is such a firm. Using only a small labour force the company has concentrated upon making special purpose plant machinery for use in quarrying and mining. One of the numerous machines this company has developed is a brush boat, that is a machine for cleaning the hulls of super tankers and other large bulk carriers. This has since been sold to large shipping companies all over the world. Another interesting piece of machinery the company has successfully manufactured is 'rough terrain' handling equipment, which is to be marketed to Middle Eastern countries for use on construction sites. Gwyn Humphrey himself is responsible for all design work. Local open-cast mining activities at Llanharan have provided opportunities for the re-building of heavy equipment by this firm, whose expertise has even been recognised by manufacturers in the United States.

EDUCATION

THE earliest known school in the district goes back to the days of Cromwell's Commonwealth. It was kept by Francis Davies, the rector of Llangan, who was one of the 278 clergymen ejected from their livings by the Propagation Act of 22nd February, 1650. Davies had little private means and was forced to keep a school to maintain himself. As well as ejecting the clergy, the Propagation Act went further. As part of its policy of puritanising the people, it attempted to establish a complete system of schools for Wales. Care was taken by the Government to ensure a ready supply of funds for the establishment of these nonconformists schools and money was set aside from impropriations and tithes to pay the schoolmasters. One such school was established at Cowbridge, and surprisingly another in the remote hamlet of St. Mary Hill. We can only surmise that this was because there was a flourishing pocket of Puritanism at St. Mary Hill at that time. These nonconformist schools were on the whole short-lived, and although they paid their schoolmasters the handsome salary of £40 a year, and in some cases admitted girls, they met with only a limited success. For one thing there were too few of them and they were also not distributed evenly enough to reflect the true concentration of population.

After the Puritan experiment failed, the only schools to be established in the Border Vale were a few unendowed schools at Llanharan, Ystradowen and St. Mary Hill. One has to wait for the religious awakening of the first half of the eighteenth century before a definite attempt was made to provide some measure of education in every parish. This was achieved mainly through the inspired work of Griffith Jones of Llanddowror, and in the period 1746-1760 his system of Circulating Schools was adopted in most of the Border Vale parishes. The earliest schools were set up in Aberthin (with 109 pupils), Gelli Fedi in Peterston-super-Montem parish and Llanharry about 1747, but a few years later they had come into existence in most of the hamlets of the Border Vale. The method of running the school was a simple one. The clergyman of each parish was asked to assist and sometimes conducted the school himself. If he was unable to help, the use of his church was sought, and an itinerant teacher would be summoned to take a class for about three months at a time. The period was too short to teach anything but reading, and the Bible and the Catechism were the only text books. The schools were held in churches, farms and cottages or wherever the pupils could be accommodated.

53

Griffith Jones' educational aims were undoubtedly narrow since his chief concern was to save the souls of his fellow countrymen, and it is evident from the reports sent him by the local clergy that most of these schools achieved their intended results. This was certainly true of the school at Llanharan where in 1759 the children were 'so perfect in their reading, so as to be able not only to say the church Catechism, but also to answer the Questions in the Exposition of it, and to repeat the Responses of the Church at Divine Service, to the great satisfaction of their Parents, and the rest of the congregation . . . '. The results at the Llanharry school were even more remarkable. In the words of Griffith Jones himself, it is clear that a great change had come over the people of that parish since the formation of the school:

By an Account in the British language sent me (*i.e.* Griffith Jones) the same Time with the Letter above, it appears, that about eighteen Persons who before were common Swearers, Profaners of the Lord's Day, Scoffers and given to Drinking, &c, &c were greatly reformed by Means of this School, who behave now as become well-disposed and serious Christians, praying GOD to bless the Welsh Schools and the charitable supporters of them.

At the start of the nineteenth century the provision of education in the Border Vale, as elsewhere in the country, was deplorably poor. There were a few private adventure schools here and there such as those kept for young ladies by the Misses Culverwell at Cowbridge. Another private day school was kept at Llanharan by John Miles, a well educated farmer. Daniel Owen, a squire of Ash Hall, attended this school in his youth and in an article 'Wales Sixty Years Ago' written about 1894 he tells us that for some offence or other he was made to stand with one foot on a stool and hold a poker above his head until his limbs hurt. In the Pencoed district there was another private venture school at Ballarat. Its headmaster was 'Siencyn Ty Charles' and farmers' sons attended it from as far afield as Mynydd-y-Gaer.

Next there were the dame schools, which in most cases were supported by the local church or gentry who usually guaranteed the dame a minimum wage, in addition to what the parents could afford to pay her. There are two interesting accounts of the local dame schools at Penllyn and Llanharry in the infamous Reports on Welsh Education of 1847. At Penllyn the Commissioners found that the school was entirely under the superintendence of Dr. William Salmon of Penllyn Court. He guaranteed the dame ten pounds a year besides the penny a week she took from the children. Miss Homfray of Penllyn Castle apparently helped the girls of the school by supplying canvas and materials for different articles of clothing, which were awarded as prizes for good conduct. The children had to attend service at Penllyn church and for this each child was given a penny a month by Dr. Salmon.

The Report of the Commissioners of Inquiry, as is well known, painted a black picture of the state of Welsh education at this time. But there is little doubt that, with exceptions here and there, the majority of schools deserved the adverse criticism directed against them. The schools were held in badly lit churches, chapels, cottages or inns, while the books and teaching equipment was pitifully inadequate. The masters and dames were untrained, underpaid and only a step or two ahead of their pupils. They were a motley crew of injured soldiers and sailors, sextons, paupers, etc., while some were forced into teaching by some disability like blindness or loss of limb. One such master was an old pedagogue called Hopkins, who ran the *Bear Inn* school at Llanharry about the year 1870. A journalist writing about him in the *Glamorgan Gazette* in 1926 tells us he was eighty years old:

He hardly had the ability of his Tonyrefail contemporary, and certainly not his irritability, except on rare occasions, when Twmi'r Teilwr's shop had run out of snuff, which the old master kept loosly in his capacious waistcoat pocket. On such occasions, the pupils, many had whiskers, and not a few of whom are alive to-day, said he was a very devil, and a terror to be near. The school was kept in the club-room of the Bear Inn, and was often visited by the dear old Rector of those days — Rev. W. Williams — who was deeply attached to the younger children, whom he seldom or never failed to regale liberally with apples from the Rectory orchard, or sweets from the village shop, if apples were out of season. By arrangement, or otherwise, the gentle Rector's welcomed arrival generally meant an opportunity for the old pedagogue to pop into the adjoining inn for a wee drop of the elixir of life, yclept chwys-y-ci. Hopkins was a firm disciplinarian, but the Rector had but a very vague notion, if, indeed, any such, of discipline, and would not have hurt a fly. When the cat is away the mice will play, and while the master was at his class, the little school became a Bedlam, and dogs, cats, and birds gave it a wide berth, so terrific was the noise. The Rector walloped one of the tables which served as desks, with his walking stick, and shouted for silence at the top of his voice, but the more he walloped and shouted, the more the uproar grew, till the pedagogue's tool-box hat appeared passing the window towards the door, when silence reigned supreme instantly. In reply to the master's inquiry about the children's behaviour in his absence, the Rector's invariable reply was,

55

'Very fair, on the whole, Mr. Hopkins'.

Schools of this sort had no fixed summer holidays, so the children had to revert to a time honoured custom of locking the master out of school. By hook or by crook the pupils induced the master to venture out of the building, then windows were sealed, doors bolted and barricaded with desks and benches, and when the master demanded entrance it would be allowed only if he conceded six or seven weeks holiday. Negotiations through the keyhole between the master and his pupils would be long and boisterous until a compromise as to the length of the holiday could be reached and an undertaking guaranteed by one or two influential onlookers that no one would land in hot water over the rebellion.

Although the National Society was founded in 1811, it built no schools in the area until much later. In 1839 a National School was

Performance of 'The Fairy Chain' in the 1920s by pupils of the 'Mountain School,' Llansannor

built in Cowbridge and another was opened in 1862 at Pencoed and used the church premises. The headmaster was a Mr. James and the attendance was voluntary. Unfortunately many of the poorer families could not afford the charge of a penny a week. Other National Schools established in the area were those at Llansannor in 1872 and Pontyclun in 1880. With the passing of the Education Act of 1870 several Board Schools came into being. One of the earliest in the district was set up at Llangan in 1876. It provided for

70 children and its first headteacher was Mrs Emma Evans. The Pencoed Board School was opened a few years later in 1879. Mr. Hughes of Penllyn was appointed headmaster at £60 per year in addition to his house and coal. Another such school was established in Miskin village in 1875 at a cost of £1,841 6s 2d for 252 children.

The primary schools which served Llanharan and Llanharry are of a later date and therefore are given separate treatment. Llanharan for much of the nineteenth century had no day school but in 1860 a Miss Thomas arrived from Blackmill to open a tiny little school in an upper room above the village smithy near the Square. Miss Thomas was a skilled needle woman who attracted pupils from all the neighbouring villages. She was succeeded by John Smith, affectionately known as 'Bugs'. During his time as headteacher, the school moved to premises near the Church for a while, then in 1892 Llanharan Primary School was built in Chapel Road. With the development of coal mining at South Rhondda colliery at the turn of the century, it was found necessary to build a junior school at Brynna in 1904. Its first headmaster was D. Emlyn Davies and a Mrs. Elizabeth Davies was his assistant. An interesting extract from the log book of 21st February, 1941, records that the school was closed because of damage done to the premises by an enemy bomb. From 1940 to 1945 the school took in evacuees from

Dolau School. Llanharan. Standard V, 1931

Llanharry 'Tin' School, 1913

Rainham School, Gillingham. Stan Stennett, the well-known comedian, attended the school for a while when living at Ty Robert farm. A third school was built at Dolau, Llanharan, in 1928, which was said at the time to possess the finest buildings and equipment in all Wales and the West of England.

The children of Llanharry meanwhile had no school of their own, and received their education at the 'Mountain School', Llansannor, for many years after the *Bear Inn* school had closed. Older inhabitants still recall the boy pupils spending their pennies on tobacco in Mrs. Radcliffe's shop near the *Collier's Arms* on their way to school. About 1912 Llanharry parents began to complain about the distances their children had to walk and petitioned for a school of their own. At first the Peniel chapel vestry was used but in 1913 the Tin School was built. This was a small building consisting of two classrooms, a hall and two cloakrooms only. Conditions at the school were very primitive. It was far from comfortable and in winter everyone huddled around the huge open stove. Once the inkwells were literally frozen solid and had to be placed around the stove to melt. In 1935 a modern Primary School was built and its first headmaster was David Rees.

The first steps to provide secondary education in the Border Vale occurred in February 1931 when the Pencoed Senior School was opened to give education to the age range 11-14. It was only the second of its kind in Glamorgan. Since then several more second-

Llanharry Junior School, 1960

ary modern schools have been built locally. Recently, comprehensive education has been established at Y Pant school (Lower
School to Bryn Celynnog) in 1972 and Pencoed in 1973. After a
period of much controversy the Cowbridge Grammar School and
Girls' High School were also replaced by a comprehensive school
serving a rather smaller 'catchment' area. Without entering into
the debate over the pros and cons of comprehensive education, we
can say with certainty that Y Pant school near Talbot Green has
pioneered the way ahead in progressive education. The prefect
system was scrapped in 1968 in favour of a School Council with
pupil representatives from each form and two staff members. Since

Llanharry Council School, 1935-36

Enud Lloyd and Stephen Harvey of Y Pant Lower Comprehensive School meet Princess Anne, President of the 'Save the Children Fund'

1964 the school has an adopted ship through the British Ship Adoption Society; first the *M. V. Llantrisant* under Captain Dixon of Pontyclun, but now *M. V. Willowbank* under Captain Rees of Cardigan. Since 1972 the School had been a branch of the 'Save the Children Fund' and has two adopted children, Monika in Austria and Rizawanulla in India. In recent years three pupils, Angela Tudball, Enud Lloyd and Stephen Harvey, have had the honour of being presented to Princess Anne, the President of the 'Save the Children Fund' in recognition of the school's efforts. In 1973, the school won first prize in the Secondary Schools' Section of the 'Wales in Bloom' competition, and the pupils were delighted when invited by the local council to take part in large scale tree-planting on Llantrisant Common as part of a Conservation Scheme.

In recent years it has become increasingly obvious that the children who desired a bilingual education in Glamorgan were far more numerous than had been anticipated. In 1960 only 80 pupils were receiving this kind of education, but by the seventies that number had increased to such an extent that a third bilingual secondary school was needed in the county and it was decided to open one at Llanharry in 1974. Since the boundary changes

Pupils of Y Pant taking part in tree planting on Llantrisant Common as part of a Conservation Scheme

brought about by the reorganisation of local government there are now two bilingual secondary schools in Mid Glamorgan at Rhydyfelin and Llanharry, and one in West Glamorgan at Ystalyfera. From now on Ysgol Gyfun, Llanhari will grow rapidly by taking in about 200 children annually to the first year classes.

PETERSTON-SUPER-MONTEM

PETERSTON-Super-Montem, as its name implies, is an upland parish separated from Llanharan by the tributary brook called the Ewenny Fach. It was formerly a chapelry or hamlet belonging to the parish of Coychurch. The church, whose ruins can still be seen on Mynydd Portref, was dedicated to St. Peter. This is a later dedication than the Celtic ones so common in the Border Vale. It is Norman and reflects the influence of St. Peter's Abbey, Gloucester, at that time. St. Peter's day is commemorated on 29th June.

In the Middle Ages, the boundaries of Peterston for the most part coincided with those of the manor of Newlands, which was an early acquisition of the lords of Coity. In 1631, it was part of the Sidney possessions in Glamorgan, but there is no evidence from the surveys that any coalmining was carried on as at nearby Llanharry. Probably the seams were too deep to have been exploited at this early date. There was no copyhold land, but the 1631 survey of Newlands does state that there was a corn mill situated on the

Llanharan Mill, mentioned in the 1631 survey of Newlands Manor

Photograph: Haydn Baynham

Ewenny Fach in the village of Llanharan. The old mill, occupied by Mrs. Ethel Wetherall and sons today, is clearly the oldest known house in Llanharan village. The last of the jolly millers were John and Edmund Rees before the mill was closed in 1908.

Before the sudden growth of Brynna in the closing decades of the last century the parish of Peterston contained no village at all. Its pattern of settlement consisted of the Hendre-Wen mansion, some scattered farmsteads of great antiquity, two mills, a few cottages near Llanharan village and the derelict church of St. Peter's, higher up on the hillside.

The old church, described in a book by Edward Lhuyd as 'a ruinous thing till of late yeares' had stood for centuries on the ancient ridge road that ran from Llantrisant to Margam. The fugitive King Edward II must have passed close by in his abortive attempt to escape his enemies in 1326. The church, set amid splendid mountain scenery, was always popular with the bards of Glamorgan. It was still in regular use in the eighteenth century; in the years 1736 to 1740, fourteen marriages were performed there, one more than at Coychurch. At this time the churchyard was the meeting place of people other than for worship. It appears from the following extract from the Quarter Sessions held at Neath in July 1731 that 'certain ale drapers from Cowbridge were fined 6d. each for selling ale, ginger bread and cakes in the churchyard of Peterston-super-Montem on the Lord's Day'. The festival known as 'Gwylmabsant' — a revel or wake often in riotous form — was held at Llanbad until it was suppressed by the fiery eloquence of David Jones of Llangan, the well known Methodist preacher. In time a new church was built in Brynna, and the chalice, bells and registers were transferred there. In recent years, annual services have been

Bethlehem Chapel, built in 1781 on Coed Bychan Farm

conducted on the site of the old church but it is sad to reflect that thoughtless ramblers have desecrated the old gravestones.

The Congregational Chapel known as Bethlehem, which stands today in the south eastern corner of the parish, was established in Peterston in 1780 almost by accident. The cause, which had begun on Llanharry Meadow in 1730, had moved to the house of Richard Watkin, yeoman, in Llanharan by 1758. Amicable relations existed between the dissenters and the Squire of Llanharan William Powell, for he granted them a public house in the middle of the village, which was converted into a chapel. On the death of William Powell, a hardening of attitudes occurred between the new Squire, the Rev. Gervase Powell, and the dissenters. He turned the congregation out of the chapel and they were forced to obtain some land on Coed Bychan farm in Peterston parish to build a new chapel which they called Bethlehem. It has remained the spititual home of numerous families in the locality for nearly two hundred years. It was rebuilt in 1836 and grew in strength, particularly under the ministry of the Rev. William Griffiths of Treoes and Bethlehem (1830-1867). His two nephews Samuel Miles and William Holland were active deacons at Bethlehem in the early years of the century and other descendants are still involved in its affairs. T. J. Witts in his book *'The Forgotten Years'* tells how during the religious revival of 1905-6 a village football team arrived at Bethlehem chapel after a match still dressed in their kit to attend a service.

The estate plans of Hendrewen are the best starting point to trace the history of the coal mining community of Brynna. As early as 1815 there are coal pits shown near Nant Ciwc, to the west of Gelli Fedi Mill. Brynnau Gwynion is shown as an area of open waste land, which then extended as far westward as the present village centre of Brynna. The only building in Brynna in 1843 was the *Eagle Inn*. It had got its name from the crest of Richard Turbervill of Ewenny who in the middle of the eighteenth century had acquired the Hendrewen estate by marriage to Florence Lougher. The crest was an 'eagle displayed sable, armed and wings tipped or'. The period 1881-1901 saw Brynna mushroom into a thriving mining community alongside the *Eagle Inn*. This era was dominated by the exploitation of the South Crop of the South Wales coalfield at a number of local collieries and drifts, Brynnau Gwynion, South Rhondda and Hendrewen among them. Of these South Rhondda was by far the most important and the sinkers' huts, sixteen in number, were soon Brynna's first settlement within the sound of the mine's hooters. As colliers flocked in from the Forest of Dean to inherit the long terraces of houses at Southall, William Street and Church Terrace, they rapidly made inroads into

Brynna F.C., 1954

the Welsh way of life, until today very few Welsh speakers are left.

For its size, Brynna has an astonishing sporting record. In the *Eagle* hangs a portrait of an unbeaten rugby side of bygone days called the 'Drainpipes'. But it is in soccer that the village has really distinguished itself. Composed almost entirely of colliers, Brynna United has had many successes especially in the immediate post war period. In 1945 the team became Welsh League Champions (Western Section). Two years later, it won the Welsh Challenge Cup, beating Lovell's Athletic, no mean team, at the Welfare Ground, Llanharan. But their finest hour came in 1949, where at Bargoed they won the coveted South Wales and Monmouthshire

Evan Bowen, Individual Champion of Pencoed and District Darts League, 1959, 60, 61

Amateur Cup beating Brecon Corinthians 3 goals to 2. That famous side was composed of the following players: Fred Bird, captain, George Merry, Tommy John, Hedley Tomlins, Wynford David, Wyndham Johns, Dick Roberts, Percy Smith, Geoff Powell, R. Travers and Clive Rossitter. Another versatile sporting character from Brynna is Evan Bowen. Evan, who played Welsh League First Division football for Caerau, has the unique distinction of having won the Pencoed and District Darts League singles title on no less than twelve occasions.

LLANILID

THE early history of the parish is steeped in romance and fantasy. The church of St. Ilid and St. Curig, which today stands isolated in the fields, is without doubt an ancient foundation, the result of some early Christian missionary effort in the Border Vale. There is a tradition — found in the Triads — that Llanilid church is the oldest church in Britain. This tradition talks of a visit made to the Welsh prince Caractacus (Caradog) at Llanilid by none other than St. Paul. The Apostle had earlier met Caractacus in Rome about A.D. 58-59 when they were both prisoners. Furthermore, Brân, the father of Caractacus, was at the time of Paul's visit being held at Rome as a hostage for his son. Brân later returned to Llanilid bringing with him several missionaries, including St. Ilid himself. As a result of Ilid's missionary efforts in these parts,

Edward Williams ('Iolo Morganwg'),
1747-1826

Photograph: National Library of Wales

Llanilid church is said to have been built. Controversy has surrounded Ilid over the centuries. Iolo Morganwg, in particular, produced elaborate stories about him, and even went so far as to suggest that Ilid was an alternative name for Joseph of Arimathea, thus linking his beloved Vale with the Glastonbury Grail legends. Iolo had such faith in his inventions that in 1800 he went to visit

Llanilid and wrote in his diary: 'Excursion to Llanilid church, behind it a large Tumulus. Tre Fran the habitation of Bran Fendigaid, The Tumulus, possibly the original pulpit'. These words give us the clue why Iolo chose obscure Llanilid as being the site of the earliest British church. He was prompted by the remains of antiquity in the neighbourhood such as the fine Norman motte near the church, and he found at Llanilid the place names Trefran, Ffynnon Garadog and Bryn Caradog, which prompted him to invent these details. Modern scholars, however, as we have shown in an earlier chapter, are inclined to the view that Christianity came to South Wales in the wake of the Romans.

However much one argues about Llanilid being the seat of Christianity in Britain, it cannot be disputed that the church of St. Ilid and St. Curig is indeed a very old and mysterious building. The only genuine clue as to the antiquity of the church lies in the ancient foundations at the foot of the north side of the nave. Mystery also surrounds the name of the church. Modern scholars have suggested that the word Ilid simply refers to the name of a district as in the names of Llandaff and Llandovery. It is also rather odd that the church seems to have been rededicated when the Normans arrived in Glamorgan. Rhys ap Iestyn, Lord of Ruthin, gave the church of Llanilid with its land to Neath Abbey, and in a list of the possessions of Neath Abbey, dated 1208, it is called the church of St. Ilith or Illid. Yet a few years later it is referred to as the church of St. Julitts.

The present building is a neat, Victorian edifice. Surprisingly, it was in a ruinous condition throughout most of the last century. In 1881, a wide appeal was made to restore it, and to quote the church guide book 'when £380 had been collected work was begun, as it was felt another winter's weather would have disastrous effects'. Of particular interest inside the building is a Norman font bearing a crudely executed trefoil design, a holy water stoop, a piscena and the door and stairway which once led to the Rood Loft. What catches the eye in the churchyard are the two yew trees which are said to be hundreds of years old. One of these trees has an oak and mountain ash tree growing out of its centre, a result probably of a squirrel hiding an acorn in the hollow of the tree. The stone stile in the wall was built for the weary pall-bearers to rest their coffins on after carrying them the long distance from the road. In a nearby wood is Ffynnon Ceri, the rag well we have referred to earlier, which was used until recent times by the local farmers to draw their water. Among the pieces of church plate are a Georgian silver chalice 'dedicated to the Parish of St. Julit' in 1760, a paten dated 1691, and a pewter alms dish.

Relics of the past are plentiful enough in the vicinity of the

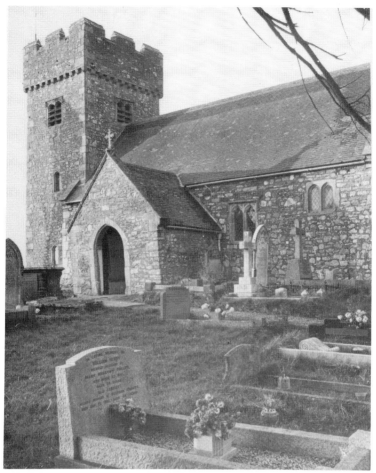

Llanilid Church   Photograph: Haydn Baynham

church. The earthworks to the south have often been described as a Roman marching camp, but it is more likely that they are a Medieval moated site, with a wet ditch originally filled from the brook which flows close by on the south. It is possible that there was originally a timber-framed hall within, replacing the one that stood inside the ring motte. The motte itself is a very fine one, situated on land which rises up on the south bank of the Ewenny Fach. The mound is 15 feet high and nearly 100 feet in diameter.

The thousands of guests who wine and dine with mine host Mr Roderick at the *Old Mill*, Felindre, probably do not realise the associations that the site had with the crusading Knights of St. John of Jerusalem in the Middle Ages. Until a year ago the ruins of an old mill stood alongside the *Fox and Hounds*, but when Rural Inns Ltd. took over the old pub, they incorporated the ruins into their ultra modern establishment. The mill was the focal point of a corn growing manor belonging to the Hospitallers called Milton, which was one of their chief possessions in Glamorgan. When the Order of St. John was dissolved in 1540 John Thomas Bassett of Bonvilston obtained the manor by purchase, and in his will, dated 1551, part of his property is described as: 'A water mill . . . in Mylton, called Grete Mill, and Manor of Milton'.

It is obvious that the manor of Milton was not restricted to Llanilid parish, since it also included a place called 'Sanctuary' as far east as Saintwell in the parish of Caerau, near Cardiff. This Sanctuary seems to have been a hospice and in an age much given to pilgrimages, it is possible that at Felindre many foot-weary pilgrims may have rested on their way to St. David's, Pembrokeshire.

By the seventeenth century the lives of the hundred or so inhabitants of the parish came under the control of absentee landlords. By 1666 three powerful landowners, David Jenkins of Hensol, Humphrey Wyndham of Dunraven and Robert Thomas of Llanmihangel had acquired most of the land. By the eighteenth century, well over a third of the parish belonged to the Llanmihangel estate. The most important family in the parish were the Meyricks, who appear from the parish registers to have been very prolific. No less than sixteen baptisms of their children are recorded as having taken place between 1714 and 1731. The registers also reflect the full cycle of life among a peasant community. Usually they are uninteresting records of births, marriages and deaths, but occasionally they are enlivened with such remarks as 'Hard Frozen winter in ye Year 1739'. The same names recur in each generation, but English names also crop up such as Palmer, Radcliffe and Plummer. Illegitimacy appears to have carried little stigma in the eighteenth century, and seems to have been rife among the peasantry. For instance, in 1762, eight of the ten baptisms were of children born out of wedlock, and this in a population of little more than a hundred. In a period of land enclosures, the resulting poverty must have caused couples to postpone marriage as long as possible, with the inevitable results.

In such a scattered and entirely rural parish, a vigorous social life must have been difficult to achieve. The chief meeting places for centuries have been the well, the smithy and mill. In former times the parish extended northwards over the hills, and the farmers of Tyn-y-Coed, Llanilid and Coed Elai were always on bad terms with the rate collector who had to tramp the mountain to receive the rate in threepenny bits and coppers. Schools are good focal points for any community, so it was unfortunate that one was never established in the parish. In 1847 the children attended a day school at Penprisk, and even as late as 1920, the Morgans of Trefran, the Theophiluses of Pantiscoed and the Davids of Fronwen had to walk in foul weather and fair to the Mountain School, Llansannor.

Since 1851 there has been a steady decline in population as families have moved away to the industrial belt. Open cast coal mining has thrust Llanilid into the twentieth century, and although the scars of industry will one day be healed, one doubts whether the old atmosphere of this charming parish will ever return.

LLANHARAN

BEFORE it became one of the most thriving of the village communities on the south crop at the end of the last century, Llanharan was a charming village of moderate size situated on the confines of the Border Vale. Of the church of St. Julius and Aaron little is known before 1563 when it is first mentioned. As we have said earlier, it is dedicated to Julius and Aaron, the first Welsh martyrs, who are commemorated on 22nd June. The church was, according to Archbishop of Wales C. A. H. Green, part of the Tewkesbury possessions in Glamorgan about 1180. In 1563, it is described as a chapel annexed to Llanilid and to have in it 'christening and burying as a parish church'. The original church in the early nineteenth century was thirty four feet long and contained ninety sittings. It was rebuilt in 1858 or 1859 by J. Rees, the grandfather of Madam Jones-Leyshon of Llanharan and Mardy. It is thought by many of the older inhabitants that the present path through the churchyard was the aisle of the earlier building. There is an interesting reference in the church records that the sexton of 1700 received sixpence for every grave he dug, providing the deceased was buried in a coffin, otherwise he received fourpence.

In the Middle Ages, Llanharan belonged to the Welsh lordship of Ruthin. The Welsh did not yield easily to the Norman advance in these parts, and we read in G. T. Clark's *Limbus* that in the hamlet of Garth Maelwg two carucates of land worth annually £2. 6. 10½d. were utterly laid waste in the reign of Henry III. The nucleus of the Llanharan estate, however, cannot be traced earlier than 1652, when it was the inheritance of one Jevan ap Rees. He is undoubtedly the same person as Evan Rees, gentleman, who is listed in 1666 as one of the chief freeholders of the manor of Ruthin. Part of his property, known as Ton-y-Gof, can be identified as an area of land around Llanharan House, and he may be regarded as one of the first Squires of Llanharan.

The will of Evan Rees is a fascinating document. In it he bequeaths 'two shillings to repair of the church of Llanharan', and he gives ten bushels of oats to be made into oatmeal for the poor of the parish. The inventory of his will is also detailed enough to show that he lived in a fairly comfortable, well stocked seventeenth-century home, though there is no silver plate.

The nucleus of the Llanharan estate did not remain in the hands of the Rees family for long: by 1694, Robert Swinglehurst, son of Richard Swinglehurst, rector of Llanmaes, had bought the property. In his will, dated 10th March 1701, Swinglehurst bequeathed all his messuages and land in Llanharan to his sister Alice Hopkins of Gwern-y-Tarw for life and after her death to his nephew Rees Powell of Llangynwyd, who had already acquired a foothold in Llanharan village. It is recorded that he leased the Corner House in 1700 to Gwenllian Griffith, widow, for 99 years.

We have already told the remarkable story of the rise of the Powells and the building of Llanharan House in an earlier chapter. One of the most hard headed of this grasping eighteenth-century family was the Rev. Gervase Powell, who was a noted figure in the social life of Bath in the days of Sheridan. In fact, there is an intriguing suggestion that Margaret Powell, Gervase's wife, was none other than the original Mrs. Malaprop. David Jones of Wallington, who obtained his information from the Nicholl family of Llantwit Major, quotes a typical malapropism attributed to Mrs. Powell. 'A turpentine walk through a scrubbery is a very nice reproach to a house'.

After the death of the Rev. Gervase Powell in 1795, the Llanharan part of his estate was bought in 1806 by Richard Hoare Jenkins of Pantynawel for £11,000. Richard Jenkins, unlike the ambitious Powells, was an uncomplicated, warm-hearted country squire, to whom fox hunting and the preservation of game was as important as public affairs. Squire Jenkins was acclaimed as one of the chief sportsmen in South Wales, and during his lifetime Llanharan became a famous village in the field of hunting, attracting London sportsmen to Llanharan House for three or four months at a time. Squire Jenkins began to acquire a taste for the chase early in his life for he and a Mr. Price of Pentyrch managed to get a few harriers together while they were at Cowbridge Grammar School. They kept them in a small outhouse behind the *Duke of Wellington*. Having taken possession of Llanharan House, Squire Jenkins lost no time in starting his first kennel of hounds and engaging 'Shoni' Harry as his huntsman. It is recorded that he bought drafts from twenty-one different packs, and his packs hunted fox, hare and otter over an extensive countryside from Llantrisant to Cowbridge. He was a 'beau ideal' of an English gentleman, and oppression was unknown on his estates. In 1831 he was made High Sheriff of Glamorgan, and in his official capacity he had to arrange the execution of Dic Penderyn the working-class leader of Merthyr. Richard Jenkins privately believed that Dic was innocent and regarded his own involvement as the most detestable duty he ever had to perform. When he died, in 1856, poor folk and cottagers from a wide area turned up in droves, to pay their final respects to a well-loved landowner.

After the death of Squire Richard Jenkins, the Llanharan estate after an interlude passed to John Blandy Jenkins (1839-1915) of Kingston Bagpuize, Berkshire. Local administration was his ruling passion. For thirty-eight years he was a member of the Bridgend and Cowbridge Board of Guardians, and for twenty years (1895-1915) was Chairman of Glamorgan County Council. He served also as a District Councillor, was a member of the Court of Quarter Sessions, and a leading member of the County Roads and Bridges

Mr. and Mrs. Harry Skevington

Authority years before the County Council took over its functions. In 1912 he was presented with a marble bust of himself on the occasion of the opening of the new Glamorgan County Hall in Cathays Park, Cardiff. It is still preserved in County Hall.

It was during the latter Squire's early years at Llanharan House that one of Llanharan's most humorous characters came to reside in the village. He was Harry Skevington, who left his native Derbyshire in the 1870's to live at Tyn-y-Pwll cottage on the Bridgend Road. He was often to be seen tidying up the gardens of Llanharan House, and apparently Col. John Blandy-Jenkins took an immediate liking to him. He was employed as a labourer and was such a familiar figure in the district with his horse and cart collecting the household refuse that he was dubbed 'Skevy the Scavenger'. Harry had one or two friendly encounters with the Squire in the convivial atmosphere of the *High Corner Hotel*, but he always seems to have had the better of the Squire. T. J. Witts in his *Forgotten Years* includes the following amusing anecdote about Harry, who had caught the Squire's eye in a meeting with local farmers at the hotel:

'What will you have to drink, Skevington?'

'What are you drinking, Squire', was Harry's reply.

'Whisky', replied the Squire.

'Then I'll have the same as you, Guvnor', grinned Harry.

Harry retained the friendship of his social superior all his life and on the death of the Squire in 1915, Harry Skevington was chosen to lead the funeral procession. Harry Skevington's drinking habits were notorious in his youth. Nine times out of ten his pony would make its own way home from the *High Corner* to Bridgend Road unaided, with Harry helpless for drink in the back of the cart. Strange to say, Harry changed his way of life as he grew older. He became one of the founder members of the Bible Christians (Methodists), whose first meetings were held in a loft over the blacksmith's shop.

The last three decades of the nineteenth century saw an intensive development of coal mining, especially at Meiros. This pit, which flourished from 1870 to 1931, was easily the most important to be developed on the south crop. In its early days Solomon Andrews, one of the proprietors, used to make unexpected visits and set all the workforce astir. At one time the pit employed over eight hundred men. Later, as Meiros declined, the Powell Duffryn pit which had been sunk at Bryncae in the early twenties grew in importance. At this pit a revolutionary technique known as horizon mining was successfully employed until unfavourable geological conditions closed it in 1962.

During the era when King Coal reigned supreme over the destinies of Llanharan, the times were hard and the disputes between masters and men were bitter and protracted, yet an incredible host of colourful and eccentric characters was thrown up to stimulate and amuse their fellowmen. One such character was Dewi Haran, the merry and convivial host of the *New Inn*, which in the nineteenth century stood on the site of Trotman's shop in Chapel Road. 'Jack of all trades, master of none' might well have applied to poor Dewi, who was in turn tailor, poet, publican, lecturer, farmer, chandler and auctioneer. Tailors in Dewi's days were peripatetic and walked from house to house throughout the district and at each house worked sitting cross-legged upon a table to make suits for half-a-crown a day. Having become landlord of the *New Inn*, Dewi found life no easier, especially as the mill shoemakers were notoriously poor-payers. So poor Dewi conceived the craziest of notions. He would build a grand hotel with a hundred bedrooms on the site of the sulphur well on Garth Maelwg and sell the drinking water for a penny a glass. The scheme naturally fell through as did most of Dewi's hairbrained ideas, but he did later achieve considerable fame as host to a brilliant gathering of bards and musicians at his auctioneer's office in Taff Street, Pontypridd.

Dewi's prophesy that Llanharan would one day become famous as a spa ironically came true a few years later. So popular did the sulphur wells become that they attracted visitors from as far afield as London and Birmingham, and the farms in the neighbourhood were crammed with guests right through the summer months.

Not all the characters associated with the coal industry were male. Before the South Rhondda and Meiros pits were in full production, Sallie Mulsod and her five donkeys were to be seen daily supplying the needs of the village from the mine on Llanharry Meadow. More recently, in the early years of this century, Llanharan had its own coal roundswoman in the person of Ann Thomas, or 'Annie Baltic' as she was most frequently called.

Mrs. Ann Thomas ('Annie Baltic')

Annie's feats of strength and stamina were unbelievable when one considers what is demanded in coal delivery. She used to start her working day as early as 4 a.m., summer and winter. With her pony and cart she would proceed to the goods yard at Llanharan, load up unaided and deliver around the neighbouring villages of Llanharry, Pontyclun and Pencoed as well as her own village. She would always leave five bags of coal on the side of the road, opposite Brynawel on Llanharry Meadow and incredible as it sounds today, the bags would be untouched until she collected them a week later. Her pony would pull into the *Fox and Hounds*, Llanharry as if by instinct and would always be given a tot of ale. On her rounds Annie would also sell sand from Merthyr Mawr to the local inns to be sprinkled on the floors.

Once the influx of newcomers from the Forest of Dean and the West Country was absorbed into the community, it did not take the people of Llanharan long to create their own forms of entertainment. Choirs, sport, brass and comic bands began to enrich the lives of ordinary folk and help them to escape the harsh realities of the mining landscape. The Llanharan eisteddfod, in particular, enjoyed a pride of place in community life fifty or sixty years ago. It grew to be one of the largest in South Wales with as many as forty choirs competing in the main choral event and singing to several thousand people in a huge marquee in the Welfare Ground. One of the earliest Llanharan choirs was formed about 1905 under the

Rees Thomas's early choir with Madam F. Jones-Rees, their accompanist

leadership of Rees Thomas and was fortunate in having Madam F. Jones-Rees as its accompanist. This choir was often to be heard performing in the grounds of the Big House in front of the Blandy-Jenkins family. Another well loved choir was that of David Hughes, which won the first prize at Aberdare on twelve successive occasions. In 1966 a new choir was formed at the Llanharan Rugby Club under the leadership of the late Vincent Witts. This choir with a lighter repertoire than the earlier ones has enjoyed a

Llanharan R.F.C. Songsters, 1972

tremendous success in the local clubs, chapels and welfare halls. It has done much charity work over a wide area and once sang in front of thousands of admiring listeners in Woburn Abbey. Its present conductor is Tudor Benjamin J.P. and the accompanists over the past ten years have been Mrs. Olwen Williams and Mrs. Moffat.

Llanharan's cultural achievements are not restricted to choral singing alone. In the early years of this century, the village boasted a fine brass band led by Fred Pick, a 'Forester', who left his native Cinderford to become its conductor. His son, Ron 'Doc' Pick, inherited his father's musical talents and became one of the best traditional jazz trumpeters in the locality in the forties and fifties, forming his own dance band called 'The Ambassadors'. The festivities attending the miners' holiday period were always a highlight of Llanharan's social life and prominent on these occasions was a colourful comic band called 'Buster's Barnstormers'. This hilarious group of funny men, led by Vincent Witts, were frequent performers throughout most of the valley towns and villages. In 1948 at Port Talbot they were acclaimed the 'Champion Comic Band of South Wales'.

We shall probably never see the likes again of men such as Jack Watkins, 'Ruffy' Woodland, Bill Witts, Ted 'Griffo' Evans and Will Stallard, who provided hours of endless pleasure to packed audiences on the Welfare Ground. The leader of the Barnstormers,

Buster's Barnstormers', Llanharan's Champion Comic Band

the late Vince Witts, deserves a special mention: Vince, popularly
known as 'Buster', was the originator of the band and for many
years the successful conductor of the Rugby Songsters. He was one
of Llanharan's most popular personalities and his sudden death in
December 1975 evoked this warm tribute from County Councillor
Joseph David, one of Llanharan's senior citizens:

'Vince was born in the same village as myself, and I have had
the pleasure of knowing him all his lifetime. He was an outstanding character and artist in his own right. His life, though
short, was full and active and he used his wonderful talents
to provide happiness and joy to countless people, including the
sick and handicapped as well as children and the elderly in
their concerts and festive occasions. He was an asset to our
community and will be sadly missed by all who knew him.'

Llanharan has a fine sporting tradition with rugby football well
to the forefront. An old photograph of an 1898 village team on view
at the local rugby club is one of the earliest rugby prints in the
district. As miners flocked in to Llanharan to work in the Meiros
and South Rhondda collieries some notable family links were
forged with the local club, with the Cogbill, Shellibeer, Pascoe and
Russell families well represented. At one time six Cogbill brothers
played in the same side. The club has had more than its fair share
of star players, and international honours have been accorded to
Danny Pascoe in 1923, Garfield Owen with six caps in the 1954-5
season, and Eynon Hawkins with six internationals for Wales at
Rugby League. The club has introduced modern intensive coaching

79

Llanharan R.F.C., late 1940s

methods and trainer Mervyn Davis has proudly seen a whole crop of youth internationals blossom forth, including Barrie Baxter, John Morgan and Trevor Worgan.

In the sphere of boxing, three men have written their names in the book of fame. They are Charlie Bundy (the 'Carnera of the Rhondda'), Sid Worgan and Ron Pritchard. Charlie Bundy, who acted for a while as a sparring partner to Jack Petersen, is a perfect example of a 'hungry fighter' serving his apprenticeship in the small-time booths of the Rhondda Valley. He fought the redoubtable Tommy Farr on three occasions, losing narrowly in each encounter. His draw with Eddie Phillips at Cardiff in 1935 and his remarkable encounter with Bruce Woodcock, in which he

Llanharan R.F.C.. 1957/58

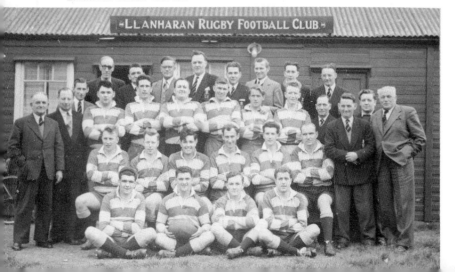

floored the rising star with a terrific right-handed punch, will always be recounted in the annals of Welsh boxing. Sid Worgan's rise to fame as a featherweight was quite sensational. He suddenly hit the headlines in 1941 by cleverly outpointing 'Kid' Tanner of British Guiana, the world's number two ranking featherweight and lost narrowly to the immortal Nel Tarleton. He won the Welsh title in 1944 and in a career of over two hundred fights he lost only half a dozen or so. Today Sid Worgan is the popular landlord of the *Bear Inn*, Llantrisant, and is much respected in the district. The third boxer, Ron Pritchard, was a bantamweight of great pugnacity, who in his one hundred and seventy fights drew large crowds wherever he performed throughout South Wales.

Numerous other people have in their different ways helped to put Llanharan on the map. William Jenkins of the Mill bred a remarkable strain of spaniel which found its way as far afield as the U.S.A. in the Victorian era. In recent times, Councillors Joseph David and Cliff Lewis both became Chairmen of the Cowbridge Rural District Council, with Councillor David being the first ever to receive the jewel and chain of office. The Bryncae sisters Sandra and Dawn Cater have both won a 'Miss Wales' title and according to Eric Morley of the Mecca Organisation, created a unique record of sisters winning the title in successive years.

In the field of literature, Tegwen Lewis' compositions have long been familiar to a wide range of readers throughout South Wales. Brought up at the footstool of Wil Ifan, she published a remarkable collection of poems under the title of *A Singing Mountain Farm*. Miss Lewis' roots are to be found in the past of Llanharan, where her grandfather was a minister of religion, and there is a marked literary strain in her family. Her aunt Mrs. Sarah Holland Miles wrote a history of local traditions called *Dros yr Ysgwydd* (*Over My Shoulder*), while her sister Mrs. Mehefyn Williams, Llanharan's ever popular librarian, has displayed her literary talent in farming magazines. Of Miss Lewis' poetry, A. G. Prys-Jones, the well known Anglo-Welsh poet and critic, has written: 'These collected poems bring to us the unhurried rhythms of nature's seasonal rise and fall, the sounds, sights and movements in brush-wood, meadow land and bracken and the warm, homely atmosphere of the farm house.'

Several other writers from Llanharan have published works in the last few years, mostly of historical interest. George Williams, the industrialist who lives at Llanharan House, himself a former High Sheriff has published an excellent history of the High Sheriffs of the County, while at the end of 1975 Terry J. Witts wrote a full-length history of Llanharan, interspersed with many first class photographs, which he entitled *The Forgotten Years*.

81

As the village becomes ever more conscious of the traditions built up in the past, it is pleasant to conclude with the news that the Taff-Ely Borough Council's Planning Committee have agreed to a recommendation to set up a conservation area in Llanharan. The main character of the original settlement near the High Corner comes from its dignified architectural style and the attractive material used in the buildings, which have remained largely unaltered over the years in their random arrangement along the banks of the ewenny Fach. It is proposed to create two distinct 'sub areas'; a bustling, commercial centre around the Square, and the peaceful precincts of church, mill and schoolroom, whose rustic charm echoes back to a bygone age.

PENCOED

THE parish of Pencoed is situated about 3 miles north-east of Bridgend and covers about 2,000 acres. It is for the most part low-lying and is drained by the River Ewenny, but to the north and west the land rises towards Cefn Hirgoed and Coed-y-Mwstwr. Before the coming of the South Wales railway in the middle of the nineteenth century Pencoed was a straggling hamlet about a mile long strung out along the road from Bridgend to Llantrisant with the majority of houses concentrated at Penprysg. The only place of worship was Salem chapel and the few Anglicans in the parish had to attend the parish church at Coychurch. There was a woollen factory at Cwrt Gwilym, a malt house at Hendre and the main estate was at Tregroes, now the home of Mid Glamorgan College of Agriculture and Horticulture.

Very little is known of the early history of Pencoed. We can safely assume that the poorly drained soils of the Ewenny valley deterred early man from settling in the locality. However, there is some evidence of prehistoric activity in the limestone caves at Coed-y-Pebyll in Coedmwstwr woods. In 1884 the caves and rock shelters were explored by John Storrie, the curator of the museum at Cardiff. He discovered a number of bones and teeth and a rough flint flake. Recently a barbed and tanged flint arrowhead of Bronze Age has been found in the caves.

In the Middle Ages, Pencoed belonged to the lordship of Coity. One of the earliest references to the place is to be found in a deed of Ewenny Priory dated 1303, in which Payn de Turbervill, the lord of Coity, made a grant to the monks of 'firewood in his woods of Le Rugge (Cefn Cribbwr) and of Penkoyt (Pencoed)'. We also know that Penprysg was famous for its quarrying of freestone from at least Elizabeth I's reign. The large house at this time was Tregroes, which for most of its history belonged to the Thomas family. They are descended from the Rev. Robert Thomas who was rector of Coychurch for over 50 years. In 1662 the Rector's grandsons were involved in a famous affray on Cefn Hirgoed, during which one Edward Thomas of Coity was killed. Three of the brothers were forced to flee abroad, to Leyden, Ireland and Portugal. The eldest son Robert, who was a surgeon, was later able to return and in 1669 received the royal pardon. His son Edward managed to recover the Tregroes estate and married the heiress of Pwllywrach,

Tregroes, now the home of the Mid Glamorgan College of Agriculture and Horticulture
Photograph: Haydn Baynham

Ann Morgan, and had seventeen children. Two of their grandsons became High Sheriff in 1772 and 1777. Today the house serves as a focal point for agricultural education for the three new counties comprising Glamorgan. The Principal of the College is D. J. W. Jenkins, B.Sc (Hons), AGRIC. The farm, which occupies some 230 acres and incorporates the old Bryncwtyn farm, provides a base for successful commercial production on a scale sufficient for the teaching of crop husbandry, animal husbandry, mechanisation and farm management.

The oldest place of worship in Pencoed is Salem chapel, which was built in 1775 and in June of last year celebrated its bicentenary. To mark the occasion, the Rev. William Owen, the

Salem Chapel, Pencoed
Photograph: Haydn Baynham

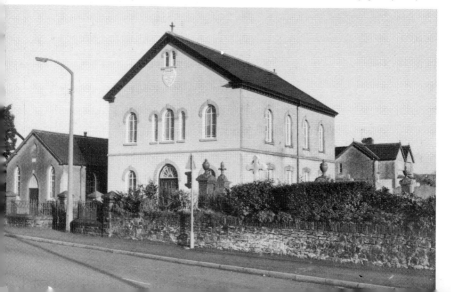

present minister, published a fascinating history of the chapel. Salem was born in the flames of the Methodist Revival and owes its origins mainly to the efforts of the fiery Rector of Llangan, the Rev. David Jones. When the little society which met regularly at Tresaeson expressed a wish to build a permanent meeting place, David Jones threw himself wholeheartedly into the task of collecting enough money during his preaching tours of England and Wales. During the years 1774-1779 he collected the sum of £282-3-7½, including a donation of a guinea from King George III's coachman. He regularly attended a fellowship service on Sunday mornings at Salem and his wife, Sinah Jones, is buried in the chapel burial ground.

One of the oldest houses in the Pencoed district is Cwrt Gwilym. Records show that when the Penllyn estate was divided in 1546 Christopher Turbervill was awarded certain properties which included the manors of Penllyn and Llangan and a tenement called Court y Gwillim. In the nineteenth century it was owned by Jenkin Morgan of Pencoed and in 1814 a lease was granted to David Jones and his heirs for a period of 50 years at a yearly rent of £20. During this period it was used as a woollen mill and an inventory of 1848 contained the following items:

'3 old engines, viz:

One tucker, One Scribbler and one carding engine, worth £5.'
Daniel Jones, the grandson of the original lessee, could not negotiate a satisfactory renewal of the lease and moved to Aberkenfig in 1864 and built a water-powered woollen mill on the site of an old grist mill on the River Ogmore, two miles north of Bridgend. He married Mary Thomas of Tan-y-lan, St. Mary Hill, who was a sister to the Williams family of Ty Candy, who are mentioned separately in this book. Since 1864 the property of Cwrt Gwilym has had various owners, including Job Chatterton, Pencoed, Thomas Evans Tor Coed, Arthur Evans, Brynffrwyd in Coychurch, and finally Trevor Jones the present owner.

Another old farm in the vicinity of Pencoed was Bryncwttin Here lived the Howell family and one of its members, David Howell, kept a most interesting Account Book giving detailed records of all kinds of farming routine in the early part of the nineteenth century. As he acted for a while as highway surveyor for the hamlet of Pencoed he has recorded entries of the payments made for haulage of stones to repair the Heol-y-Porth Mawr, now known as Felindre road. In 1810 he paid Thomas Merchant for hauling 44 cranmuck of stones from Penprysg quarries the sum of £2-2-4d, while David Morgan was paid 12/- for six days work at Penprysg quarries. Thomas David was paid 3/9 for stones at 3d a cart load.

The Britannia Hotel, opened in 1850, the day the first train ran through Pencoed

Photograph: Haydn Baynham

The year 1850 was the turning point in the history of Pencoed for during that year the South Wales railway passed through the village and a railway station was constructed. It is said that the *Britannia Inn* was opened on the day that the very first train ran through the village. Coinciding with the coming of the railway was the exploitation of numerous collieries along the southern outcrop of the coalfield, starting with the opening of Cribbwr Main in 1850. The earliest mines were worked at Pencoed as elsewhere by the 'Pillar and Stall' system in which stalls were driven off the level headings ten to fifteen yards apart and for a distance of about 50 feet along.

The convenience of rail communications and the growth of mining soon brought small scale industry to the Pencoed district. In 1878 E. David, a Coity blacksmith, opened the Pencoed Foundry, where colliery equipment was made including trams, tools and pit cages. About forty blacksmiths and moulders worked here in the early days and in the 1920's over 120 men were employed in manufacturing over a hundred trams per week. Pencoed has always been famous for its clay pits and in the latter part of the nineteenth century John Williams of Durban Villa, Pencoed, founded the Pencoed Brickworks. At its peak the company was able to supply at least 30,000 bricks per day to all parts of South Wales. One is fascinated to learn that the Birmingham Town Hall was faced with Terra Cotta bricks from Pencoed. Unfortunately the clay pits became flooded about 1900 which in time spelt the doom of the company.

Throughout the nineteenth century as the population rose from 490 in 1851, to 1,179 in 1901, religious, social and sporting activities began to grow. In 1862 the National School was opened, followed by a Board School in 1879. Nonconformist chapels were also built during the years after 1850. The Penuel Baptist was erected in 1862, but the Welsh Congregationalists held their early meetings in the *King's Head* hotel until a chapel known as Bryn Seion was built in 1898. Trinity Presbyterian Church held its first meetings in the Council School, but eventually a site was found for a chapel in 1897. We have already mentioned the *Britannia*, but there were several other inns at Pencoed at this time. The oldest was the *Crown* which was situated below Salem chapel. Later the *Old King's Head* hotel and the *Groes Inn* appeared. The *Groes* was soon renamed the *Railway Hotel* and was kept by the Chatterton family for over 70 years. Much of the social and sporting life of Pencoed have been centred on the *Britannia* within the last seventy years. At the turn of the century a 'ladies only' club was practising Women's Lib well ahead of its time. Other organisations to use the famous 'long room' included the Pencoed Ladies Choir, the Pigeon Club, the Pencoed and District Dart League, the Pencoed Rugby Club and the local miners' lodges.

From the early years of this century Pencoed's famous Silver Band had practised in the long room of the *Britannia*. Some of the first bands were Brass Bands which were formed in 1902 under a Mr. Moore of Cardiff and again in 1912 under R. W. Lewis of Pencoed. After 1928 Charles Sloper became bandmaster and many fine concerts were given in the locality during the days of economic depression. Under the leadership of Ivor J. Owen from 1946

Pencoed Silver Band with its conductor Mr. R. W. Lewis in the early 1930s

Pencoed Royals Jazz Band

competitive training commenced and in the period 1948-50 many cups and trophies were won. Other conductors have included Frank Wareham, Edward Clark and Len Davies. The band is very much a family affair. For example Len Harris the landlord of the *Britannia* for many years has had a son, two grandsons and a grand-daughter all playing in the band. Several past players have won great distinction in the field of music. Evan Ll. Watkins as an eleven-year-old in the 1930's won a cornet solo in the National Eisteddfodd and rose to become the Director of the College of Music, Southampton.

The 'Pencoed Royals' have also done much to put Pencoed on the map. Founded in 1957 by Bert Simmons, Gwilym Evans and Albert Chilcott, this well known girls' Jazz Band has won practically every local championship at one time or another. Reformed in 1970, they soon became Welsh Junior champions in 1974 and were among the finalists in the World Championship at Alexandra Palace in the same year.

The post-war development of industry in the area, notably in the large Tremains Industrial Estate, has attracted many people to settle in Pencoed and a series of privately owned estates have been established. At present there are 760 children attending the Pencoed Junior and Infants' School, and a second junior school known as Croesty Primary School was opened in 1967. On 5th July 1973, a fine new Comprehensive school was officially opened by County Councillor W. E. Board, replacing the old Secondary Modern. The Secondary School has produced some fine rugger players and in one season alone Alan Henson, Jimmy Cooper, Wayne Hall, Steven Harris and Anthony Creiger all played for Bridgend Rugby Club. Other pupils who have brought honour to their school are Alan Bird and David Edwards, who won International schoolboy caps for Wales, P. L. Jones, and Steven J. Harris the 400 metre County Champion.

ST. MARY HILL

IN Medieval times the parish of St. Mary Hill lay in two manors, those of Gelligarn and Ruthin. In Gelligarn the clergyman was always styled a vicar, having the vicarial tithes only, while in Ruthin he was in the position of being a rector. In the twelfth century the manor belonged to Samson de Halweia. He belonged to a family who were the hereditary butlers or cup bearers to the lord of Glamorgan. Samson de Halweia, as we have seen, was worried by the Welsh raids from the north and gave Gelligarn to Neath Abbey in exchange for property in Devon. It remained with Neath Abbey until the Dissolution of the Monasteries and their important grange was sited where the ruins of the Court are today. It was sold after the Dissolution to Sir Rice Mansel and after a generation or two it passed through marriage into the Aubrey estate.

St. Mary Hill church is an ancient building and consists of chancel, nave, south porch, with a modern embattled western tower. The font is Norman and so is the chancel arch which is inserted into the north wall of the nave. In the *Glamorgan County History*, volume 3, a reference is made to the piscena with a double drain and also to a low relief canopied aumbrey in the chancel at St. Mary Hill which suggests the skill of a woodcarver of the

St. Mary Hill Church   Photograph: Haydn Baynham

Middle Ages. In 1254 the 'church of St. Mary near Gelligarn' was valued at one mark. By 1291 a separate vicarage had been established worth £2. The church plate includes an Elizabethan chalice with a cover dated 1576. The fine medieval cross lay in ruins by 1887, but was restored by Sir Thomas Mansel Franklen of St. Hilary. Once the task had been completed the grateful parishioners of St. Mary Hill presented Mrs. Franklen with a beautiful ink stand and candlestick.

The farm houses of the parish are very ancient; in the ruins of Tresaeson for instance Jenkin Williams of Pencoed found a very old stone fireplace with beautiful carvings, circles, stars and a cross which probably dates back to the thirteenth or fourteenth century. He presented it to the National Museum of Wales. St. Mary Hill Court, on the site of the old medieval grange, is a house of seventeenth century date with an early eighteenth century addition at the south end. An outbuilding to the south of the house is probably earlier, and incorporates stone framed doors with bull-nose stops. The other important old houses of the parish are Craig Ruthin and Pant Ruthin, both of which are houses of the late sixteenth century and have fireplace stairs. Another interesting old house of somewhat later date was the *Bell Inn*. It is one of the many local inns which have vanished from the Border Vale over the past seventy years or so. The *Bell* originally stood opposite the church. Like the *Morning Star* Pentremeyrick and the *Crack Inn* near Cowbridge, the *Bell* was much frequented by poachers in the last century and consequently had something of a bad reputation. It is said that on the day of the great horse fair, the takings at the inn were so large as to see it through the rest of the year.

Ty Candy mill, situated in the picturesque Ewenny valley between St. Mary Hill and Coed y Mwstwr, is another building worthy of mention. The mill was built in the seventeenth century and appears to have been in the same family for most of its history, with the names changing as it sometimes passed through the female line. The census of 1851 mentions a Morgan Williams, miller and farmer. He farmed 78 acres in addition to operating the mill. Morgan Williams was the great grandfather of the Thomas family who are in Ty Candy now. Until just after the First World War, Ty Candy was a bustling place and the grandfather of the present occupants is still remembered as working day and night during the Great War grinding flour and animal feeding stuff for the local community. Farmers usually went to the mill once a week delivering their grain and collecting their flour. At the turn of the century the miller charged by the bushel for his services, but before that he had always kept back a portion of the grain in payment. The mill wheel, which can still be seen today, is at least 15 feet in diameter.

An interesting description of St. Mary Hill in the early nineteenth century can be found in Carlisle's *Topographical Dictionary* of 1811. 'The Fair is holden on the Down . . . chiefly for Live Stock, woollen and linen Drapery, and Pedlery. This parish contains about 860 acres of Land; of which, about 150 are open Downs, constituting a sweet and healthy Sheep-walk, for a fine-woolled breed of Sheep; and 40 acres of Woodland; and all the rest have been enclosed from time immemorial'. Walter Davies writing about the same time was equally enthusiastic about the downland sheep. He wrote: 'Many of these wastes, especially those of St. Mary Hill,

A Ruthin Chapel outing about 40 year ago

in the Vale of Glamorgan and Cefn y Bryn Hill in Gower, produce the sweetest herbage imaginable, and the sheep grazing there are remarkable for the fineness of their wool and the excellency of their mutton'. On the summit of St. Mary Hill mountain are some enormous sandstone boulders which have a very striking appearance from a distance. In the last century these stones were of considerable importance to the farmers of the locality for they used them to sharpen their instruments of husbandry such as hooks and scythes.

No chapter on St. Mary Hill would be complete without a brief mention of Ruthin chapel which for most of its ninety years has been closely associated with Salem, Pencoed's well-known Welsh Presbyterian church. It was built in the 1880's by Jonathon Howells, a retired Cowbridge merchant, who intended the little conventicle on the hill to be used by all Christians, irrespective of their denomination. Howells was a man well ahead of his time and his dream soon came to nothing. However, when the chapel was threatened with closure, Salem chapel took it over as a schoolroom in 1890 and later as a sort of 'chapel of ease' for the Methodists living on Mynydd Ruthin. Later the chapel was recognised as a church in its own right, but has always shared a minister with Salem.

LLANGAN

THE parish of Llangan is about 1,200 acres in extent and lies north of the main Cowbridge-Bridgend road in pleasant farming country. Of the two villages, Llangan has the more straggling appearance and is sited at a lane junction on a low hill about 4 miles east of Bridgend. The village has an informal character and its buildings are of various ages with most of them having slated roofs. On the outskirts of the village stands the ancient parish church of St. Canna, which with its Celtic and Medieval crosses and rectory stand in a pleasant grove of trees. Treoes is also of great antiquity and is a perfect example of a street or ribbon village.

In the Middle Ages Llangan was bound up manorially with Penllyn for it appears from the old records that Penllyn, Llangan and Goston (Treoes) were associated together from the period of the Norman conquest of the Vale of Glamorgan. Around Treoes and Llangan lay the open fields of the manorial system, and each farmer would have several scattered strips of land. When the strips were eventually hedged they became narrow enclosures and these can still be seen 'fossilised' as it were within the modern field system. Several roads ran out from Treoes into the open fields and they marked off the open fields from the common meadow. The corn mill for the three manors of Penllyn, Llangan and Goston was built on Treoes moors, and it was called Moor Mill. It is still possible to trace the old routeway Heol-y-Millway which ran all the way from Penllyn to this mill.

Llangan holds a very special place in the history of Methodism because it was in this parish that the Rev. David Jones created a hive of religious activity in the eighteenth century. He was born at Aberceiliog in Carmarthenshire C 1736. His maternal grandfather had been the vicar of Llandysul and had married a wealthy Jewess. This would probably explain David Jones' pronounced Jewish features. David's parents hoped he would take up farming, but an accident of childhood completely altered the course of his life. One day as he was playing in the kitchen of the farmhouse the lad fell into a vat of boiling milk and was lucky to escape with his life. After this accident it was decided that he would no longer be strong enough for farm work so would enter the Church. The great preacher later in life would often refer to his childhood accident

92

David Jones of Llangan

claiming that he bore the signs of his calling upon his back.

After ordination he soon established a reputation as a powerful preacher and came to the notice of the Countess of Huntingdon, the great patroness of Methodism. She persuaded her friend Lady Charlotte Edwin to present him to the living of Llangan to which he was inducted in 1767. On his arrival he found the standard of morality and religion at a very low ebb and energetically threw his heart and soul into a revival. Soon the unknown little church became the Mecca of the Border Vale as huge crowds gathered to hear him preach in the churchyard and even in the barn close by. On the Communion Sunday it is said that the congregations were so large that water had to be used instead of the communion wine. Although David Jones resisted a dissent from the church until his death in 1810, that break was an inevitable one. Throughout the nineteenth century the tide in Llangan parish as elsewhere in the Border Vale swung inexorably towards nonconformity. In 1848 the Visitation Returns tell us that the majority of parishioners belonged to the Independents and Methodists and in the 1851 Religious Census the curate fo Llangan noted:

'This parish for the last 8 or 10 years almost wholly given up to Dissent, is chiefly Welsh. For the last two months or nearly so 2 services have been performed in the church by order of the Diocesan'. The nonconformist cause had been started in Treoes in 1831 by William Griffiths, the minister of Bethlehem chapel, Llanharan. The first church was formed in an old barn in the village. The old building and garden were purchased from Edward Mordecai of Treoes for £30 and in 1841 Saron Chapel was built for

Saron Chapel, Treos　　　　　　　　　　　Photograph: Haydn Baynham

£240. On 30th March 1851 there were 140 worshippers present at morning service, 91 in the afternoon and 300 in the evening, and after the religious revival of 1859-60, it became necessary to erect a gallery.

As regards education in the parish it appears that the vestry of Saron Chapel was the first school in the nineteenth century. Here an exciseman called Truman 'spared not the birch of which he never kept fewer than half a dozen'. He is supposed to have been related to President Truman of America. According to Dan Thomas of Church Farm, Llangan, there was another private school held in one of the outbuilding of his farms. Here a local cobbler taught the village children while he worked. In 1874 a school Board of five members was formed for the United district of Llangan and St. Mary Hill and in 1876 a Board School was erected. The present school was built in 1911.

It is interesting to note that the parish of Llangan was the birthplace of two famous nineteenth-century Welshmen. John Pritchard, the architect who was responsible for the rebuilding and restoration of Llandaff Cathedral, was born there in 1817, while David Howell ('Llawdden') the famous preacher-poet and Dean of St. David's originated from Treoes.

94

In recent years Treoes has started to come to terms with the twentieth century. In 1936 mains water was introduced to the village and electricity came about 1950. A village hall was built about six or seven years ago, and with the rapid development of

Llangan Council School, October 1922

private housing there are going to be more people likely to use it. A newly formed Women's Institute, a boys' and girls' youth club, a weekly disco and a thriving Sunday school at Saron are the growing signs of a healthy community life for the years ahead.

PENLLYN

THE parish of Penllyn lies for the most part on a crescent-shaped limestone ridge and is about 1,800 acres in area. Apart from the moors to the east there is hardly an acre of level ground, and the castle from a height of 450 feet dominates the landscape for miles around. It is not surprising that in bygone days the castle served as a sort of barometer for the neighbourhood. As Iolo Morganwg wrote:

> When the hoarse waves of Severn are screaming aloud,
> And Penlline's lofty castle's involv'd in a cloud;
> If true the old proverb, a shower of rain
> Is brooding above and will soon drench the plain.

There is some evidence of prehistoric activity to the south of the parish, especially in the neighbourhood of Pentremeyrick. A few hundred yards across the road from Cross Farm are the 'Humpty Dumpty' mounds, which are the remains of an ancient British

A Romano-Belgic pottery tankard found near Pentre Meyrick

Photograph: National Museum of Wales

homestead — possibly a chieftain's residence with some farm buildings. It was occupied in the period just before the Romans came. Cattle, pigs, sheep and horses were kept and were an important form of wealth in the Iron Age. Some of the Belgic pottery found at this site might have belonged to the followers of Caractacus who fled from the Romans into this region.

The church called Llanfrynach stands in lonely isolation in the far corner of the parish and is the only dedication to St. Brynach in Glamorgan. Because of its isolated position Iolo Morganwg postu-

96

Llanfrynach Church　　　　　　　　　　　　Photograph: Haydn Baynham

lated the existence of a village of Llanfrynach, which he claimed
was destroyed by Owain Glyndwr in 1404, but we have no support-
ing evidence to substantiate this. The present church is a Gothic
building of crude workmanship, and it has a massive square tower
and a saddle-back roof. The rood-loft stairs remain as do the solid
stone seats which are found on both sides of the inside walls. Here
in the Middle Ages the aged and infirm were allowed to sit while
the more able-bodied stood at the centre throughout the service.
Near the yew trees in the churchyard is a headstone which reads
'In memory of Rees Morgan of this Parish, died 7th April 1816,
aged 103.' About one hundred and fifty years ago tradition has it
that the bells of Llanfrynach were stolen by the men of Coity. A
feud of long standing resulted from this act and up to the time of
the First World War the youths of both parishes would fight each
other annually at St. Mary Hill Fair over the ownership of the bells.
By the nineteenth century the church had become a near ruin, but
fortunately it was much restored by Dr. William Salmon of
Penllyn Court about 1841. The chapel-of-ease in Penllyn village has
been used for regular services since about 1750.

Penllyn castle was sited strategically by the Normans on the edge
of the Border Vale to cover the Welsh lordships of Talyfan and
Ruthin to the north. Only a few vestiges are left of the original
Norman castle and they include a fragment of the early square
keep behind the present house and some interesting stretches of
herring-bone masonry, dating from about 1100 at the base of the
keep.

By about 1126 the manor of Penllyn belonged to Sir Robert le

97

Norris and it was run along feudal lines similar to manors in the Vale of Glamorgan with free and unfree tenants working in the open fields, which were situated near the present village and also at Treoes and Llangan. The Norris family held the manors of Penllyn, Goston and Llangan until 1320 when the line ended. Through four heiresses the manor was divided among the Turbervills, Matthews, Stradlings and Kemeys, but the Turbervills kept the castle and the larger share of the manor. Later the castle passed through various hands including members of the Seys, Stradling and Mansel families until it came into the possession of Lady Vernon who bequeathed it to her friend and companion, Miss Emelia Gwinnett. In 1804 Donavon refers to Miss Gwinnett's 'new' castellated mansion', so it would appear that the house in its present form would appear to date from this period. Finally, further interior alterations were made to the house by John Homfray in 1848.

In the eighteenth century large crowds used to visit Penllyn to see its great curiosity, a gigantic elm tree in the farmyard of Trevychan (part of Llwynhelig farm). It had been hollow for years and years, but had a head of fine branches. A wager was made about the year 1790 as to how many of the stoutest men in Cowbridge could squeeze inside the tree and drink a stated number of gallons of ale. It seems that the challenge was accepted as twelve very stout men managed successfully to squeeze inside the tree and consume their fill of ale to the amazement of many onlookers. However, when David Jones of Wallington passed by years later in 1881, he wrote of the elm 'it was a dreadful wreck, its noble head had disappeared and nothing remained but its shorn and hollow trunk'.

A remarkable young doctor named William Salmon came to

Dr Salmon's Well, Penllyn   Photograph: Haydn Baynham

reside at Penllyn Court a year after the battle of Waterloo. He had married Hester, the co-heiress of Major Reynold Thomas Deere, and after this splendid match the young doctor ended his practice and settled down to the life of a country gentleman. Dr Salmon greatly improved the Penllyn Court estate, landscaping it with a large number of trees and managing his two vineries. He built his own laboratory and often entertained great men of science like Michael Faraday who always received a basket of grapes during his visits to the Court. Dr Salmon was a generous benefactor to the people of the village who particularly appreciated the gift of the two wells provided for domestic water supplies. The wells are found by the Court near the roadside and in the last century a large brass cup was secured to the masonry, but it has long since disappeared. A journalist tells us that the Jubilee Year of 1887 was noted for its drought and scores of people from as far afield as Colwinston, Llysworney, Llansannor, St. Mary Hill and Llangan carrying buckets, jugs and other vessels used to queue up for hours around the precious wells. Dr Salmon lived to become the grand old man of the Vale and when he died aged one hundred and six years on 10th May 1896 he was said to be the oldest person in Wales and the oldest doctor in Europe.

Penllyn is a parish rich in folk lore. It seems that in the nineteenth century the woods around Penllyn castle had the reputation of being inhabited by winged serpents, who terrified the local populace out of their wits. An aged inhabitant told Marie Trevelyan that in his youth the winged serpents were described as very beautiful and 'looked as though they were covered with jewels of all sorts'. He said that their existence was real and not a story made up to frighten the children. David Jones of Wallington had also heard of the serpents and informed us that a Penllyn man in his father's service used to horrify him in his youth with seemingly true accounts of the slaughter of one of these creatures. Then there was the well known 'Penllyn cow'; whenever there was a plentiful supply of anything, people in the Border Vale used to say 'It's like the Penllyn cow'. It appears that a compassionate lady of the village kept one of her cows solely for the sake of the poor. The cow was milked daily by the needy and in time the creature grew venerable and was regarded throughout the neighbourhood as almost sacred. The cow always gave an enormous supply of milk, and when milked day or night she never failed to oblige.

We have already mentioned the little Methodist chapel that once stood on the Graig. Here the spiritual needs of the little colony of squatters on the common were administered at first in a Sunday School held in the house of Dafydd Rheinallt, one of the converts of David Jones of Llangan, but when the Limes Chapel was opened in Cowbridge in 1824, the little school was closed. After a time a Sunday school was restarted in the house of William Jenkins, the Vistla, and in 1829 the City Iscoed meeting house was opened in Llansannor. Several elderly men desired to learn to read and the job of teaching them the rudiments was given to an eleven-year-old boy, who sat on the knee of Dafydd Thomas, one of the pupils to give the lessons. Later the boy became well known in life as William Williams of Swansea. A few years later the boy's father, Evan Williams, gave some land on which to build a chapel at Penllyn. This was duly opened in October 1831.

Throughout the nineteenth century Penllyn was a bustling community, especially when the lead mines of Tewgoed were in full swing. At that time they had no shortage of public houses because in addition to the *Fox and Hounds* and the *Barley Mow* at Penllyn there were the *Morning Star*, the *Travellers Rest* and *King's Head* at Pentremyrick. The *Fox and Hounds* did a roaring trade and was renowned for its one-handed clock, which never indicated the correct time and which no one but the genial landlady, Mrs. Margaret Williams, could ever read. Some rascal whom the old lady refused a drink on trust stole one of the clock's weights. Mrs. Williams was most put out at first but at length she attached the fire tongs to the chain and behold the old clock went as before. Callers at the pub could not help noticing the tongs and many humorous comments were made, but when one of them asked whether anything of equal weight would suffice, the landlady's

Penllyn Chapel   Photograph: Haydn Baynham

reply was always 'Good lord, no, nothing else on earth could keep the old clock ticking'.

The present century has witnessed the continuation of an active social life in the parish. Until recently the wells were the focal point where people from the surrounding areas could congregate and a special open air service was held there on Victory Day at the end of the war. During the 1930's life was lived at a more leisurely pace and incredible as it sounds John Bagg, a schoolboy at the time, vividly remembers playing cricket on the middle of the A48. People like Ted the tinker, who repaired umbrellas and Eder Munden, who used to sell needles, cotton and elastic, were some of the colourful characters who enriched the social life of ordinary people and spread local gossip throughout the village. Penllyn village and the Craig were then two worlds apart, the top village was virtually owned by the Homfrays, while the Graig was much more independent. A friendly rivalry always existed between the communities and even in the carnival processions each entered its own band.

Today the whole character of the village had altered. The wells are no longer used and the school and chapel have long closed. A large residential centre had been established at the Graig and the mother tongue is no longer heard in the village hall. Only the Castle remains, dominating the landscape as always and reminding us of a more refined and leisurely age which preceded our own.

LLANSANNOR

L LANSANNOR is a small parish of about 1,798 acres and comprises the ancient church of St. Senewyr, a modest Tudor mansion known as Llansannor Court, the two outlying hamlets of Breigan and City and a number of farmsteads and derelict cottages of great antiquity. The ancient church stands surrounded by trees in the grounds of Llansannor Court. The church and court are steeped in legends most of which are related to St. Cadoc. According to one account Cadoc was murdered by a marauding band in his chapel at Llansannor, called Civitas Beneventana, while taking Mass and that his beloved people then placed his body in a silver coffin and buried it secretly. No Briton was allowed to enter Civitas Beneventana, so the legend runs, as it was feared the people of Llancarfan would try to take St. Cadoc's remains back home. If this should occur, a fountain by the rampart would have over-whelmed Llansannor and everyone in it. The other legend about St. Cadoc is that he placed all his treasures into a silver casket and dropped them into a well, and ever since on certain nights he can be seen at Llansannor seated in solitude waiting for someone to speak to him, so that he can guide them to the spot where the treasure lies.

No one has ever successfully explained the name Llansannor. The name first appears in its present form in *Valor Ecclesiasticus* (1535) and is found many times in slightly varying forms in the sixteenth century. But before 1535, the only instance where some-thing like it occurs is as far back as the twelfth century in the form 'capella St. Senwarae de la Thawe'. Throughout the Middle Ages the church was known as the 'ecclesia de La Thawe'. The church itself is an unassuming building in Early English style. It has a fine sixteenth-century porch; an old sundial, inscribed but now indistinct, is displayed above it. During recent repair work parts of some early wall paintings were discovered under the plaster of the church wall. The wall painting by the south door is in the right position and of suitable shape for a St. Christopher, sadly mutilated though it is. St. Christopher was often depicted opposite the main entrances of churches and in the Middle Ages it was believed that if a glimpse was obtained on entering and a prayer offered, protection from harm or injury during the day would result.

The arrival of Stephen Bauzan at Breigan in the middle years of the thirteenth century marked the beginning of a remarkably long family connection with the parish. The Llansannor estate has descended in the same family for over six hundred years. The family were for most of the time known as the Gwyns and even as late as 1910 their descendants, the Griffith family of Llansannor House, were still actively participating in the affairs of the parish. Of the founder member of the family, Stephen Bauzan, we know little except that he acted as Sheriff of Glamorgan to Richard de Clare on three separate occasions between 1243 and 1247. It was he who built a manor house at Breigan before he was slain by the troops of Prince Llewelyn ap Gruffydd at Llandeilo in 1257. However, there had been a community at Breigan long before Bauzan's time. It is likely that a native Welsh community of pre-Norman date had been established here on the freely drained soils of the parish.

The descendants of Stephen Bauzan were important personages in their own right. According to David Jones of Wallington no less a person than Oliver Cromwell himself was descended from one of these early lords of Breigan. Eventually Bauzan's descendants remained there until about 1400, when at the death of Jenkin Fitz Aaron the manor was divided between his two daughters, the one taking Breigan and the other Llansannor. From the Breigan heiress came the Thomas family, while from the Llansannor heiress stemmed the more important Gwyns of Llansannor Court. Earlier in this book, we traced the remarkable rise of the Gwyns. Two of them, Richard and John, became Sheriffs of Glamorgan during the reign of Elizabeth I, but the most illustrious member of the family was Francis Gwyn of Llansannor and Forde Abbey (1648-1734), who held many important policital offices including Clerk of the Council 1679-1685. He was a great favourite of Queen Anne, who appointed him Secretary of War in 1713. He was also one of the leading Tories of his day and had immense patronage and influence in the West Country where in 1705 he was reported as being 'the firebrand of all this side of the kingdom in the elections'.

Throughout the seventeenth and eighteenth centuries the Gwyns, although living at Forde Abbey in Dorset, were able through their stewards to exercise an increasing control over the affairs of their Llansannor estate. During this time the estate was scattered throughout many parishes of the Border Vale, and at Llansannor it included the Court and demesne, the Old Forest, the New Forest and Trenches together with the water mill and windmill. The water mill is still occupied today by R. J. Brown and the 'Windmill Farm' is the property of Tal Thomas, a well known local farmer. Only one family, the Trumans of Pantylliwydd, were able to withstand the increasing control of absentee landlords over the affairs of the parish. This yeoman family were descended from Trooper Thomas

Truman, a Cromwellian soldier of fortune from Northampton who rose in the Parliamentary army and came to Glamorgan under Col. Philip Jones of Fonmon. His great-grandson was Thomas Truman, the antiquarian 1713-1786 who married the heiress of Pantylliwyd and settled there. Truman is worthy of recognition as one of those who fired Iolo Morganwg's interest in the history of Glamorgan and gave him at Pantylliwydd the opportunity of studying books and manuscripts on the subject. Iolo described Truman as 'a learned antiquarian and skilful genealogist who is now in a better world than this, having left no equal behind him'.

Before 1846 the last of the Gwyns of Forde Abbey had sold the Llansannor Court estate to the industrialist, Sir Joseph Bailey, and Breigan Farm became the property of the Guests. Sir Joseph spent over £3,000 on restoring the Court and added a fine teak staircase. Llansannor at this time was a fairly self sufficient community with a working mill, a smithy, a bakehouse, two inns, the *City* and the *Carpenters Arms* at Breigan, and a whole range of rural crafts were practised on the estate. David Jones of Wallington has some amusing comments to make about some of the nineteenth-century clergy at Llansannor. One or two of them it seems were quite mad, and another, the Rev. J. F. Griffith, enjoyed more than his fair share of ale at the *City* inn: 'He was that extraordinary little man, Little Griffith of Llansannor, who was a great drunkard and quite notorious for his queer manners and eccentricities. He had weak legs and made all his escapades on horseback'. Another Rector, the Rev. Owen Jones, was a skilled boxer and was often called to the *City* inn by the landlady, the late Mrs. Barkeway, to deal with the Saturday night rowdies of the 1890's.

City Inn, Llansannor Photograph: Haydn Baynham

The Gwyn family, around whom our story of Llansannor has been woven, had not completely severed their links with the parish. The Griffiths' were left a considerable part of the estates of the Gwyns in Devon as well as some at Llansannor. They built that magnificent colonial-style residence, known as Llansannor House, now the home of Francis Hayes and throughout the last century fully participated in the affairs of the parish. It was the Griffith brothers, Francis Gwyn and John Fraunceis, who were the first in Glamorgan to illuminate their residence with electric light. This happened in 1884 and many visitors came from hill and vale alike to see the novelty. Mrs. Sweeting, the grandmother of Mrs. Barkaway, kept the *City* inn at the time and the installation of electric lights at Llansannor House brought great crowds to the *City* in that year. The Griffith brothers were very clever engineers and were willing to explain the intricate workings of the new lights to all-comers, including the U.S.A. consul.

Since about 1870 there has been a Church school in the parish. It was built by the National Society to enable children of working class parents to receive a Christian education. In its early days the 'Mountain School' was built to accommodate children from a wide area including Ystradowen and Llanharry and in 1906 its average attendance was 86.9. A very generous benefactor to the school was J. S. Gibbon of Trecastle who supplied the school with its heating system. The author of this book received his elementary education at this school and well remembers the efforts made by staff and pupils during the wartime period when its headmistress was Mrs. S. J. Saunders, B.A., of Bridgend. Large garden plots were cultivated in our 'Dig for Victory' effort and we formed a Rabbit Club, while 'Fur and Feather' shows were held in Penllyn. But the children were very loath to kill their pets to eke out the meat ration and no one made much money out of selling the pelts. National Savings was another way of helping the country and one vividly recalls the excitement when the school target of £100 was regularly reached. Toys were a scarcity at the time, of course, so one winter the children made soft toys from old felt hats and rag dolls. We had many orders and the proceeds of the sales went to the Red Cross.

LLANHARRY

L LANHARRY is a parish of some 1,629 acres and comprises the original nucleated village around St. Illtud's church, a large and rather featureless housing estate, two underlying hamlets of Tylagarw and Llanharry Meadow and several isolated farms of great antiquity.

We have already noticed how the freely drained soils found at Llanharry attracted the earliest peoples to the district from the Beaker man onwards. Most of these peoples were pastoralists, a fact confirmed by finds such as the bronze axe that Howard Hopkins of Fforest Fawr unearthed on his land only a few years

Bronze axehead from Coed y Tranches, near Llanharan, probably an import from Ireland, c. 1500 B.C.   Photograph: National Museum of Wales

ago. The people who used it probably lived mainly by stock raising and dwelt in lightly constructed huts in small forest clearings.

As we have shown, the rich deposits of iron ore have been worked at Llanharry from the earliest times, but it must not be imagined that mining ceased with the departure of the Romans in the fourth century. Professor Leslie Alcock's excavations at Dinas Powis have proved conclusively that iron from Llanharry was being smelted in the llys or court of a local chieftain in the fifth and sixth centuries. One ore sample at Dinas Powis has been identified as limonite, an ore found at Trecastle, near Llanharry.

The church at Llanharry is dedicated to St. Iltud, the founder of the fifth century monastery at Llantwit Major. But Iolo Marganwg, puzzled by the name Llanharry, tried to connect it with 'Garrai Sant O Gor Bangor'. In a list of saints which was drawn up by Iolo, we read 'Garrai ap Cewydd ap Caw Cawlwyd ei eglwys Llanarrai, Morganwg' (Garrai, the son of Cewydd, the son of Caw Cawlwyd; his church Llanarrai, Glamorgan). Even in the early days of its history, people have been puzzled by the name of the 'llan'. There is a fascinating story to be found in a twelfth century life of St. Illtud which, while narrating one of the many legends about the saint, may also be an early attempt to explain the name. This version of the story is reproduced from Gilbert Doble's *Life of Saint Illtyd:*

> One night two robbers stole S. Iltut's herd of swine, taking then from the hara where they were kept and driving them towards the woodlands. They lost their way and spent the whole night wandering round aimlessly, till at dawn they found themselves back at the place from which they had started. (They hid themselves during the day). The tired animals rested till the third hour, the swineherd wondering why they were all so sleepy. At nightfall the robbers returned to the hara and made a second attempt to drive the pigs off to the distant mountain with the same result. The patience of the King of Heaven being now exhausted, they were turned into two stones, which are still called after them, and the site of the hara still bears the name of Iltut.

The distant mountain would obviously be the Garth Maelwg, but the name 'Llechau' (stones) might have suggested the two stones. The author of a recent M.A. thesis on place names in the lordship of Tal-y-fan was also unable to explain the meaning of Llanharry. The earliest version he found was Llanhari in a document of the third quarter of the twelfth century. This he suggests is the correct Welsh form. This is the version found in the works of Dafydd Benwyn, Meurig Dafydd and Gronw Williams, all poets of the sixteenth century. It is rather interesting that he adds that the correct pronunciation is like the present day vulgar pronunciation. Hence the suggested spelling with only one 'r', for doubling the 'r' would require a short 'a' in standard Welsh phonetics. We are pleased to inform our readers that the schools of the village have adopted the original form.

When the Normans conquered the Border Vale, Llanharry became part of the member lordship of Tal-y-fan. Earlier it may have belonged to the old Welsh lordship of Ruthin until Richard Syward considered it important enough to fight against the Welsh prince of Miskin, Howel ap Meredith. It became part of the demesne land of Tal-y-fan, possibly one of the few good corn growing parts in the predominantly wooded lordship. About 1246, as a result of Richard Syward's dispute with the lord of Glamorgan, Llanharry escheated with the lordship. Aferwards Richard de Clare installed William Scurlage at Trecastle, while Llanharry manor passed either by conquest or the marriage of an heiress to the Turbervills of Coity.

Trecastle apart, most of Llanharry became part of the Coity estate by 1350 if not earlier. The manor then passed from the Turbervill family to their descendants the Berkerolles and the Gamages. Finally in 1584, through the marriage of Barbara Gamage to Robert Sidney, brother of the famous Elizabethan poet, it bacame part of the Sidney possessions in Glamorgan. Tracing the boundaries of an ancient manor is a difficult task, however. It appears from the 1631 survey that the manor of Llanharry was separated from Trecastle by a little stream called Nant Felin-Fach, from Ruthin by the commons of the Gwaun and from Tal-y-fan by a rather indeterminate boundary passing south-eastwards from Pantiscoed, through Llwynbarcud, Pant Gwyn, and Gelligneuen farms. In the east, the boundary with Talygarn coincides with part of the Morfa Ystradowen peat bog. The manor itself contained certain Welsh features such as gavelkind, but was organised along the lines of the English type manors as found in the Vale. At Llanharry, we can safely say the demesne land was at Llechau. Situated on the red, fertile soils of the trias, Llechau was probably the home farm of the manor in earlier times. There were other parcels of demesne land intermingled with the strips of the copyholders in the open fields. Surrounding the church were the large open fields in which the tenants were allocated so many strips each according to their position on the manor roll. The rest of the manor was in the hands of freeholders, leaseholders and tenants-at-will. The freehold lands had been carved out over the centuries by private enterprise from the woods and wastes that surrounded Llanharry on every side. Thus on the outer edges of the manor stood the old farms of Gelligneuen, Ty Diffrwyth, Coed-y-Wiw, Pen-y-Waun, Torgelli and Rhyd y Castell.

Associated with the old farming economy was the nucleated village, with a compact grouping of church, farmhouses and cottages. In the opinion of H. J. Randall, Llanharry more than any of the neighbouring villages of the Border Vale resembled the compact villages of the shire fee. We know little about the houses which were grouped around St. Illtud's church until 1775, when in an estate plan of that year two farmhouses, the *Bear Inn* and a group of cottages, some ruined, stood around the Church and the village green. On part of the village green was the Parish House on the exact spot where Prospect House now stands. It had been built upon a plot of land given to the parish by Sir Thomas Gamage of

Llechau Farm, known as 'the mansion house' in the reign of Charles I

Photograph: Haydn Baynham

Coity, and may well have been used as the very first village hall.

Not far away at the foot of Red Hill stood Llechau farm, which was known as 'the Mansion House' in the reign of Charles I. It is an interesting old house contrived on such a slope that it has two storeys at the upper end and three at the lower. The long stone steps down to the basement floor at the lower end are not met with elsewhere in the county and seem vaguely reminiscent of the long stone steps from the first floor parlour direct to the cellar at Llancaiach (Gelligaer). The upper section as far as the central chimney is primary and the detail of wooden doors, beams and bressummer suggest a date around 1630 or a little earlier. The lower end is tacked on as can be seen by the straight joints on both lateral walls, and is not much later than the primary house. In this house about 1610-30 may have lived Lewis of Llechau, whom Iolo Morganwg tried to elevate into one of the great masters of Welsh poetry, but it is more likely he was a bard of modest accomplishments. Today this old house is occupied by Mr. and Mrs. Len Green.

From as early as 1730, when a house on the Llanharry Meadow was licensed for preaching, the meeting houses of the Congregationalists were slowly becoming the spiritual homes of the people of the locality. By 1780 Bethlehem Chapel had been built at Llanharan and by 1802 Maendy Independent Church was established. It was in the early years of the nineteenth century that the breakthrough of Noncomformity at Llanharry occurred. The impetus came from Maendy when members of Maendy Chapel began to hold a Sunday School in the village in 1820, first in the house of one Richard Richard and then at Rhiwperra. At that time the Llanharry district

109

was noted for its ungodly games, and the young men of the adjoining villages used to meet there on Sundays to play ball. One Sunday soon after the school had started, the Rev. Shadrach Davies of Maendy approached the boys playing in the field near the present Junior School, picked up the ball when it came near him and led the astonished lads to Rhiwperra school. The school flourished and in 1847 had 70 pupils on its books, 33 of whom were under 15 years of age. Nonconformity made such an impact that it was necessary to build Peniel chapel and throughout the nineteenth century the majority of Llanharry people worshipped there.

The census returns for 1841 to 1861 show that Llanharry was in the mid century a fairly self sufficient community with a wide range of rural crafts, two shops, four public houses, a mill and a dame school run by the local church. The most impressive house in the village at that time was Ty Newydd opposite the *Bear Inn*. This was originally a late seventeenth century yeoman's dwelling, but was

Ty Newydd, now demolished

much restored in the nineteenth century, possibly by the Rev. R. P. Sidney who lived there for a while as rector of the parish. Unfortunately the old house was demolished for development purposes a couple of years ago. Another interesting old house which was greatly altered at this time was Gelli-gneuen farm on the outskirts of Llanharry village. This was originally a single roomed

110

Gelli-gneuen, a single-roomed yeoman's house of the seventeenth century

Photograph: Haydn Baynham

yeoman's house which probably dates from Elizabeth's reign. It has its fireplace alongside the entrance to the hall and is therefore a Regional type B house.

From 1850 onwards, Llanharry underwent its own private industrial revolution. On Llanharry Meadow at this time was to be found a flourishing colliery, a brick works, a coke oven and a distillery. The pioneer of this industrial activity was surprisingly a local farmer called William Hopkins of Torgelli. He was one of the first people to exploit the rich seams of the south crop in modern times. It was during his time that donkeys used to carry coal from Llanharry Meadow to supply the needs of Cowbridge, Llantwit Major and the rest of the Vale. Hopkins also brought chemical workers from Bristol to run the distillery at Rhyd y Castell.

While the Meadow colliery was in full operation, the four inns of the village did a roaring trade. But disputes about working conditions were commonplace, especially in their favourite pub the *Colliers Arms*. Often things got out of hand, so it was necessary for the landlord of the day to send down the road for the village constable, Thomas Williams of Tyn y Berllan. Williams, it appears, was known as a terror to all evil-doers. Armed with a short, stout knobstick and a pair of strong handcuffs made by the village smithy, Williams would brandish his knobstick without fear or favour until law and order had been restored. Thomas Williams also delighted to intervene in the disputes between Llanharry boys and their rivals from other parishes. The young bloods of Ystradowen when they came to Llanharry bent on courting were much resented by the locals and free fights often broke out. Thomas Williams

111

would quickly quell the disturbance and would roar above the din 'Heddwch y Brenin, the King's Peace', then, 'At them Llanharry boys, we'll teach them to come here after our pretty wenches'.

Another colourful character at that time was William Hugh, and although he had been born and bred in Llanharry he had no home of his own. There came a time when he found the very spot he was looking for on which to build a house of his heart's desire. The site he set his eye on was on the outskirts of the village just below the *Fox and Hounds*, but unfortunately the plot abutted on the Glebe land, which then belonged to the Rev. William Williams. Believing that possession was nine-tenths of the law, Willie Hugh under cover of darkness fenced off a piece of land big enough for a house and garden. But no sooner was the fence up than it was down again at the request of the rector of the parish, who was no friend of Hugh, and was determined to reclaim the property of his church. The struggle waged long and furious and several times the fence was raised only to be pulled down again by the Rector's cronies. Day after day, night after night, the feud dragged on and apparently the whole village joined in taking sides with one or other party. At last the Rector relented but only after Willie had solemnly promised to name his cottage Naboth's Vineyard after a parallel case of stolen land in the Bible. It is an interesting fact that one of the subscribers to this book, Ivor R. Day of Barry, is a direct descendant of the hero of this little anecdote.

About the year 1868 St. Illtud's church was rebuilt in the Norman style and consisted of a chancel, nave, south porch and a western turret, containing two bells. There is a fine chancel arch which may well have been associated with the roof loft in the Middle Ages. The stained east window was given to the church in 1868 by John Samuel Gibbon and in the chancel is the vault of the Gibbons family of Trecastle. The name of the present rector is the Rev. George Hurlow, who encourages regular visits to his historic church by pupils from the local junior school. Mrs. Emily Snook has been organist at the church for over 45 years.

In most old villages the local inn is found in close proximity to the village church. How long the *Bear Inn* has stood on the edge of the village green is impossible to say. We can roughly date the present building to about 1650. It was a yeoman's dwelling of the hall and parlour type. The ancient beams above the fireplace in the lounge of today were originally cut with an adze giving a scallop effect. It has the fireplace alongside the entry to the hall and is typical of a regional type house of South-East Wales. In the hall of the *Bear* is found a fine eighteenth century oven. Outside the inn a century or two ago stood a pit house where cock fighting was staged.

The old inn on the village green certainly lays claim to a rich store of historical memories of one kind or another. It is first mentioned in the Glamorgan County Files of 1753, when an inquest was held in the house of Henry Jenkin, inn-keeper, before William Gibbon of Trecastle, Coroner. In the nineteenth century the inn was the venue of the day school and also the headquarters of a flourishing friendly society called the Old Club. The society had come into being in the middle of the eighteenth century and was composed of gentlemen farmers, farmers, farm labourers and craftsmen. These societies were the forerunners of our present-day

George and William Ambury, Boer War veterans, and landlords of the Bear Inn

trade unions and did a great deal of charity work among the less fortunate. They held their meetings in the old club room and imposed fixed penalties on their members for such things as arrears of dues, sponging on the funds, absence from feasts, brawling and non-attendance at funerals. When one remembers in the days before the introduction of the hearse that coffins would be carried long distances — say from Llanharry to Gilfach — on the shoulders of four strong men, it is not surprising that the fine of a shilling for non-attendance was regularly imposed. By the end of the nineteenth century the 'Old Club' was finally wound up in face of competition from the Odd Fellows and Foresters. The *Bear* has always enjoyed immense popularity as a place for eating out. Dining out at a country inn is today a much more sophisticated

113

affair than in the days of mine hostess Mrs. Emily Ambury seventy years ago. Mrs. Ambury was famous for her home-baked bread, yeast cake and home-cured ham. Unaided by modern cooking facilities, her method of cooking was most intriguing. First she filled the crudely made stone oven with some large wooden logs. These she set ablaze and when they had all burned away she used to pull out the wooden ash with a long rake. Then came an amazingly accurate temperature test. She would bare her arm and plunge it into the hot oven. If she was able to count up to twenty-one without flinching, she knew the temperature was right for baking the bread. If she had to withdraw her hand before completing the count, then the oven was allowed to cool a little

Outing departing from the Bear Inn, Llanharry, 1948

until right for baking. A cash price list in the days of landlord Jack Ambury, just before the First World War, makes interesting reading to the many who patronise the *Bear Inn* today. Bottles of rum and whisky were sold for between 2/6 and 3/6, while brandy varied between 3/6 and 6/- according to the make. Port, sherry and claret were much cheaper varying from 1/6 to 4/- a bottle.

Space does not allow a lenghty treatment of the four remaining inns of Llanharry in the last century. In passing, however, we should mention the long association that the Evans family of Llanharry had with that other ancient pub, the *Fox and Hounds*. This latter house had, until recent times, been kept in the same family for well over a hundred years. Mrs. Elizabeth Evans took over the place in the middle of the nineteenth century and after almost sixty years as licensee retired to live with her daughter Mrs. Elizabeth Rees the landlady of the former *Colliers Arms*. The *Fox* license then passed to the old lady's grandson, Thomas Evans, and after his death in 1940 his wife carried on the business until she died several years later. The place was then transferred to her son

Members of the Evans family, licencees of the Fox and Hounds, Llanharry, for over a century

Morgan, the last member of this remarkable breed of Llanharry publicans. Mr. Gwyn Evans, the chairman of the *Border Vale* book committee, is the nephew of Mr. Morgan Evans. Another interesting piece of information about this old Llanharry family is that Mrs. Elizabeth Evans, the first licensee, attended St. Mary Hill fair for fifty years and from her marquee she served liquid refreshments to the vast crowds who used to visit the Hill in those days. Her tent was particularly popular with the bards and literary men of the district who used to patronise the marquee to discuss their works and the events of the day.

Before the present iron mine opened in 1901, Llanharry was still only a small village of a few hundred souls. The village began at the *Colliers Arms*, and adjoining the inn Philip Rosser kept a store where you could buy anything from an ounce of Queen's snuff to a sack of flour, provided you trundled it home. On the site of the present Bi-lingual School was a street of cottages called Heol Las.

Then there was a forge in Llwyn-y-barcud Lane. Apart from the Croft cottages there were no houses from the forge to Prospect House where Mrs. Hayman kept the first Post Office. Behind the church was the manor pound and in the forecourt of the *Bear Inn* cheapjacks often displayed and sold their wares. On the opposite side of the road stood Ty Newydd and Pant Gwyn farms with open fields from there to Llanharry Station.

As the village grew into a thriving community of iron workers throughout the twenties and thirties, no one person enriched life more in Llanharry with his ready wit and dry humour than Billo Rosser. Some marvellous anecdotes are told of this loveable rogue, who would devise any scheme on earth to wrangle a free drink in the bad old days. One day, Billo was standing outside the *High Corner*, Llanharan, watching a comely barmaid putting some energetic elbow grease into cleaning the windows before the pub opened. 'Bring me out a large brandy', commanded Billo, 'and I will show you an easy way to put some sparkle into those panes'. The foolish

William 'Billo' Rosser

maid readily complied and Billo drank the lot then calmly proceeded to breathe on every pane. Then thanking the misled girl, he advised her to polish lightly — and walked away with a wicked grin. Billo was a brilliant impersonator, and in the candle-lit gloom of the iron mine, he would frighten many a group of workmates having a chat on the sly by impersonating the manager. Billo was worshipped by the schoolchildren of the village especially when he told them stories about his aeroplane, which no one ever saw but everyone believed in.

A seafaring character called Jack Dawley was another who could always raise a laugh or two. He could never see eye to eye with his one-legged landlord and each time Jack had more than his fair share of drink he would sink to his knees in the middle of the roadway and offer up a prayer to heaven saying 'O Lord, paralyse his other leg and don't send the beggar any crutches'. His wife was another of those larger than life characters who just don't seem to be around these days. Mrs. Dawley lived in the Croft cottage and would put her last two shillings in the collection plate on a Sunday only to go to the Rector and ask for it back on a Monday morning. Another odd thing about her was that when pegging out her washing, she would use about twenty to thirty pegs for each garment on her line. Among the older generation of Llanharry, who will ever forget Fred Hunt of the Woodlands who arrived late so often at the iron mine that he was put by the management on full time afternoon shift. Or Tom Witto of Breigan cottage for another: Tom would settle in the *Bear* on Saturday nights until Jimmy Marshall his neighbour would call in for his father and Tom. Jimmy had his aged mother outside in an old trolley and once they reached Degar Hill Tom Witto would squeeze in with the old lady

Llanharry F.C., 1933-34

117

and shout jubilantly 'Now James, drive us to the castle'. Every inn had its character who in the days before mass entertainment made their own fun. 'Morgan in the Collier's shop' would carry six hundred weight of cement for a bet, while Lewis Jenkins, Pentwyn, drunk or sober, would stand on the floor and kick the ceiling with ease.

Soccer had always been Llanharry's most prominent sport from the days when the Pops and Flagons played on Bronwen Field before the First World War. They derived their name from the fact that they changed in the *Bear Inn* and while the older members took a glass or two of ale after the match, the youngsters drank lemonade. The Austin family seem to have contributed quite a few players to the team at that time. The whole team enlisted for the Great War and football did not resume until 1922 when a team played in the Llanharan League.

Llanharry's most successful period in soccer history was in the 1930's when they came second in the Bridgend League and won the much coveted Farquharson Cup with Farquharson and Jimmy Blair, the Cardiff City internationals, presenting the cup at Llanharan Welfare Ground. The team followed up this success by winning the Vale Cup twice running in 1934 and 1935. Today's side is an equally talented one and has recently won promotion to Division I of the Barry and District League.

Llanharry F.C., winners of the Barry Dockers Cup, 1961-62

Local elections have always been hotly contested at Llanharry. Before the Welfare Hall was built, meetings were regularly held in the part of the old village green behind the church. The first district Councillor for Llanharry was the Rev. D. Richards, Rector of the Parish. Station Terrace has provided two stalwart councillors

Coronation Procession, Llanharry, 1937

in David Harris and Mrs. Elsie Pickford. Later David Rees and Eli Light served their community for many years during wartime and afterwards. One recent councillor, T. C. Lewis, had the honour of being chosen as the Chairman of the old Cowbridge Rural District Council.

Vintage buses never fail to evoke nostalgic memories of the good old days. The many shoppers, cinemagoers and dancing enthusiasts of Llanharry will never forget those obliging brothers Cecil and Cliff Hemmings who for nearly fifty years provided the only public transport service that ran through the village. Cecil and Cliff in their boneshaking old bus would pick one up literally on the doorstep anywhere on their two hourly service from Llanharry to

Local dignitaries with Mr. Arthur Pearson, M.P. for Pontypridd, at a presentation to Mr. Lewis Jenkins, pioneer of Llanharry Labour Party, c. 1938

Talbot Green. Sacks of potatoes and milk churns would find their way on board, but no one seemed to mind. What the bus lacked in comfort, it made up in efficiency, for rather than leave any man, woman, child or pet behind Cecil and Cliff would pile them in along the gangway and on every inch of the outside steps. They knew all their customers by name and even on a Saturday night when the last bus to Llanharry was choc-a-bloc with returning cinemagoers from Pontyclun the Hemmings brothers endeavoured to leave no one behind. All too often the last bus failed to navigate

Adrienne John is crowned Llanharry's first Carnival Queen by Mr. J. Skevington Summers, September 1962

Red Hill, and the driver would either ask the courting couples to walk the rest of the way home or persuade a dozen or two of the heftier youngsters to push the vehicle over the brow.

Within the last few years as a new generation has come to the fore there has been a noticeable revival of interest in community life. A flourishing horticultural society has over the past ten years produced one of the finest flower and vegetable shows in the county. In 1972, the Llanharry Scout and Cub group was formed by Group Scouts leader Douglas Summers. He and Len Pring, his assistant, recently witnessed the selection of two of their lads to represent the Welsh team at the World Scout Jamboree in Norway. They are Robert Searle and Lyndon Williams. For the girls of the village, a highly successful Jazz Band called the Llanharry Welsh Paraders won a galaxy of cups in their first year of competition. A new band called The New Arrivals has been formed for the 1976 season.

Llanharry Welsh Paraders Jazz Band, 1975   Photograph: Haydn Baynham

The Llanharry Commoners' Association is another active body which in the 1970's is doing much the same work today as the Court Leet did in the Middle Ages. The formation of these associations were primarliy intended to set up organisations which had the ability to manage the vast areas of Common Land which exist in South Wales. At Llanharry the development of open-cast mining since 1967 had brought the Llanharry Commoners into direct negotiations with the National Coal Board. An eventual agreement was reached whereby the rights of the whole of Llanharry Common were leased to the Board for a period of winning minerals and reinstatement. This in turn has given the Commoners sufficient finance to enable them to devise a future plan for the agricultural development of the seventy-two acres of common land in the years ahead. The chairman of the Commoners is Councillor Raymond Milson and its active secretary is Harry Tooze.

In 1974, Llanharry had the unusual distinction of launching a history book. Stewart Williams' *Glamorgan Historian*, volume 10, was officially launched in front of four hundred people in the local Junior School. Guests from all walks of life heard Anne Morgan, a

nine year old pupil of the school, recite the following poem she had
written for the occasion entitled the 'Windmill of Llansannor':

With sweeping arms like a giant's claw,
A towering body of brick and stone
With a tick and a tock the grinding wheels go round,
A mighty rushing sound as the wind roars from left to right,
And you think of troubled seas,
As the mighty arms fly round, the corn is crushed like sand in the
    air,
The wooden flails creak and jerk,
And wakes the miller from his afternoon nap.
On the hill stands a house near the grinding mill,
Aptly named 'Four Winds' is this lonesome place,
What a store of memories the windmill has,
The sound of Bauzan's horses as they thundered down the cobbled
    Grippy,
With knights of Breigan riding to battle on milk white horses,
Some hand painted wagons of Tudor age,
With parasol pinks and deep rose reds,
As a statley Gwyn rides by.
The majestic mill has gone for ever,
No longer does it throw its shadows
Over dales, brooks, farms and hedgerows,
Of old Llansannor.

ABERTHIN AND YSTRADOWEN

ABERTHIN, situated one mile north of Cowbridge in the parish of Llanblethian, is a village of great antiquity. It is set in a picturesque, steep-sided valley to the north of Stallingdown. Its houses illustrate a wide range of design from Tudor to modern and in Great House it has one of the finest Jacobean dwellings in the Border Vale. The place is first mentioned in the *Book of Llandaff*, where it is called 'Ebirthun' and we can safely assume that there was a Welsh community in existence here from the earliest times. Whether it was a monastic grange farmed by the 'fratres' of a big monastic house is however open to speculation. When the Normans conquered Talyfan they created the sub-manor of Llanquian and it is likely that Aberthin was the village of this sub-manor. The manor was held by the de Wintons or Wilkins family for a long period and their name has been preserved in 'Pant Wilkin', a farm close by.

One of the earliest Methodist societies in Wales was established in a farmhouse at Aberthin in 1742 and the leading preachers of the day — Howel Harris, Daniel Rowland, William Williams, Pantycelyn, and Peter Williams — were frequent visitors there. By 1749 the Society was able to build itself a proper meeting place, but

Aberthin village with Stallingdown in the distance   Photograph: Haydn Baynham

soon afterwards a serious rift developed between the Methodists who favoured affiliation with the Anglican Church and those who stressed Dissent. There were several unedifying scenes at the chapel and many of the Dissenting party were forced to leave because the trustees had Methodist sympathies. The troubles were not yet over in Aberthin chapel as there were still some members whose dissenting views could not be accepted by the Methodists. They decided to withdraw and set up an Independent church in the neighbourhood. In 1802 they built a chapel at Maendy and in 1807 they ordained Shadrach Davies as minister. He was a stonemason and is said to have built the chapel with his own hands.

During the eighteenth century Stallingdown near Aberthin was the venue of the Cowbridge Races, which were always attended by fashionable society of the day. Here is a description of one of the races run in 1769: 'On Wednesday, the 4th of October will be run on the Stalling Down a purse of £50 — Free for any 4 years old, bred in the County of Glamorgan. Colts to carry 8st. 7lbs. Fillies to carry 8st. 4lbs. The best of three heats, once round the course'. A greater crowd puller than even the races was the occasional hanging that still took place on Stallingdown in the eighteenth century. In the sixteenth century women as well as men were hanged from these notorious gallows. This was the fate of Gwenllian verch Harry of Llansannor who, in 1570, was hanged for stealing forty shillings worth of goods from the mill of John Nicoll of St. Hilary. One of the last men to be hanged at Stallingdown was John Thomas, who was found guilty at the Cowbridge assizes of housebreaking. In fact, the infamous gallows above Aberthin so terrified the population that fathers warned their disobedient offspring with the words 'You will see Caercady before you die' — Caercady being the last place the criminals beheld before succumbing to the rope.

The parish of Ystradowen contains a small straggling village strung out for half a mile along the Cowbridge to Llantrisant Road. The church of St. Owain, a modern edifice on the site of an older building, was rebuilt in 1867. Its single bell was presented by Sir Leoline Jenkins in 1685 while his brother, Evan, gave a house and thirteen acres of land to repair the bells of Ystradowen and Llanblethian church and he directed that the surplus be used to apprentice children and relieve the aged. The name 'Ystradowen' like that of Llanharry presents many difficulties. Earlier writers have claimed that the place had derived its name from Owain ap Collwyn, a Welsh prince of the tenth century, but the only source for the connection of Prince Owain with Ystradowen is in spurious documents forged by Iolo Morganwg. The earliest reference to a church at Ystradowen was in 1291 when it was declared to be worth £4 and belong to the Chancellor of Llandaff Cathedral.

When Benjamin Heath Malkin visited the parish in 1803 he wrote about the meetings of the Welsh bards at Ystradowen under the patronage of the Jenkins family of Hensol in the early years of the eighteenth century. Unfortunately Malkin was very much influenced by the opinions of Iolo Morganwg, whom he knew well. Iolo wanted to show that the early druidic traditions had been preserved in their 'pristine purity' in Glamorgan alone, and that the bards were the natural successors of the Druids. I think one can ignore what Iolo said about Ystradowen as a centre of the druidic tradition of Glamorgan, but what about the Ystradowen eisteddfodau, which Iolo claimed to have heard of in his youth, and to which Makin obviously refers? They were supposed to have been held on 28th May and to have lasted for three or four days. The bards lodged at Ty'n-y-tywod and sometimes the eisteddfod would be held under the yew tree in the churchyard. It is difficult to believe that there is no foundation for these stories. They cannot therefore be entirely disregarded for, as in much of Iolo's writings, they probably contain an element of truth.

The principal house of the parish since the eighteenth century has been Ash Hall. The earliest owners were the Deere family, who probably came from Rhoose. Mathew Deere had his estate surveyed in 1745 and it was scattered throughout the Vale and Blaenau, with only 65 acres in Ystradowen. Iolo Morganwg, we learn, was greatly influenced in his early days as a poet by Kitty Deere, who was a niece of Mathew Deere of Ash Hall. She wrote quite a lot of English poetry and Iolo insisted in a poem addressed to her that it was she who had made him into a poet. In the late nineteenth century Ash Hall belonged to Daniel Owen who was a typical 'self-made' man of the Victorian age. He was born at Llanharan but emigrated to Australia where he made a fortune in the timber trade. When he returned to England, he became a highly successful printer and paper manufacturer, and on account of his great wealth, he was invited by Lascelles Carr to become a joint proprietor of the *Western Mail*. To celebrate the event he threw a mammoth party for his staff and their families, two hundred in all, at Ash Hall, and the description of it which appears in the *Western Mail* of 1st May 1869 gives a vivid account of those balmy days of the last century. 'After lunch some played croquet and tennis, others tripped it on the light fantastic toe, some improvised games of their own, whilst the sedater members sat beneath the trees. Cricket was played on a splendid level pasture adjoining the lawn and some capital foot races were run both by men and boys. In the evening after the speeches young folk found 'kiss in the ring' an attractive amusement and the party drove off amid cheers and expressions of good will on all sides, reaching Cardiff a little after midnight'.

Wounded soldiers at Ash Hall Hospital during the First World War

Daniel Owen was succeeded at Ash Hall by Tudor Owen and during the First World War the house was used as a Red Cross Hospital for sick and wounded soldiers with Mrs. Owen acting as a highly successful matron. After the War she was awarded the Order of the Red Cross. Our picture shows one of the first batch of Commonwealth wounded soldiers who arrived in May 1915.

Most of the farms of Ystradowen in the middle of the nineteenth century were very small, with the one exception, Llwynwydog, which had 150 acres. The Mathew family lived there and also at Ty Mawr in the village. This is a very old family who have lived in and around Aberthin and Ystradowen for centuries and are descended from William Mathew of Rhoose and Aberaman, who was sheriff of Glamorgan in 1693. The late William Mathew of Brynfedwen farm was justly proud of his coat-of-arms.

Once Ystradowen became a station on the Llantrisant and

Ty Mawr, Ystradowen

Aberthaw branch of the Taff Vale railway, the village became a hive of activity especially on the Pontypridd market days. Then all the hucksters of the district together with their cargoes of vegetables, mushrooms, nuts, poultry, eggs and rabbits flocked to the little station with their handtrucks, boxes on wheels, carts and traps and there was always a porter of remarkable strength called John John willing to assist them at the station. He was so strong that it is said he even went to the rescue of the trains which failed on Ystradowen Moor incline. In the early decades of the present century Ystradowen, small though it was, could boast of a thriving saw mill, its own cattle market, two inns, the *White Lion* and the *Tudor Arms*, a village stores kept by Mrs. Sarah Gibbon and a smithy. The smithy was the rendezvous for all the youths of the

Ystradowen United F.C., 1920-21

village who under the watchful eye of Tom Griffith would blow the fire, turn the grindstone and wield the sledge. Tom, whom they called 'the Huddy Man' on account of his quaint way of swearing would also make hoops for the small children. It is to hard to believe that forty of fifty years ago this tiny village fielded four soccer sides and now it has not a single team. After the last war with the closure of the station, the social life in the village went into decline until about ten years ago the *White Lion* Friendly Club decided to bring a little fun and entertainment into the village by organising carnivals, sports meetings and historic expeditions. Their greatest contribution was to charity and there are many worthy organisations in the Border Vale and elsewhere who have cause to be grateful to the patronage of Mrs. Ann Phillips and to the money raising efforts of Cecil Woodruffe, Dewi Matthews and their fine committee of workers.

WELSH ST. DONATS

WELSH St. Donats lies to the north-east of Cowbridge and has a population of 381. When Benjamin Heath Malkin visited the parish in 1803 he said that the village was inhabited entirely by native Welsh, but today there is hardly a Welsh speaker left. The earliest recorded reference to the name 'Welsh St. Donats' goes back to 1482, but we do not know who St. Donat or Dunwyd was. The church is an ancient building in the Early English style and it was restored in 1891 at a cost of £800. Many people have in the past visited this church to see its pre-Reformation sanctus bell and its ancient oak roof. There are only four such bells within the diocese and they were usually suspended on the eastern side of the chancel arch and rung from within the chancel. The earliest record of this church is of the Chapel of St. Donats in the year 1153, and in 1180 it belonged to Tewkesbury Abbey.

A very ancient custom practised in the churchyard of Welsh St. Donats and other neighbouring parishes was that of 'raising the summer birch'. Morgan Rhys, the Ystradowen weaver, has the

Welsh St. Donats Church   Photograph: Haydn Baynham

following account in the *Cambrian Journal*, March 1853, of this fascinating pastime:

> The first thing they did was to hoist a birch bough on Easter Monday (the birch was selected because it was the straightest of all trees). On the morning of the above day the ladies met in the churchyard for the purpose of decking the bough with ribbons, and the most honourable lady in the parish placed on it the handsomest rosette, while all the other girls contributed ribbons according to their means. When the women had finished their task of decking the birch bough, they were assisted by the men in lifting it upon the cross in the churchyard, in the presence of all the other parishioners, while the harpers were playing appropriate airs. Having thus placed it beautifully decked upon the cross, they set watchmen to guard it for four days and four nights, lest it should be stolen. For it was considered a disgrace for ages to the parish that lost its birch, whilst on the other hand, a parish that succeeded in stealing a decked bough, and preserving its own, was held up in great esteem.

We are told that this honour befell Welsh St. Donats more often than any of their neighbours. The mistresses and their maids rose at dawn on Easter Saturday to finish their work by early afternoon and then they would meet at the churchyard to begin Morris dancing to the accompaniment of a harp and a fiddle until midnight.

A rather bleak and isolated landscape is still to be found at Mynydd-y-Glew (Mountain of the Brave). This wild stretch of moorland was once believed to be haunted by fairies and hobgoblins and Rice Merrick writing in 1578 classified Mynydd-y-Glew as among the commons, warrens and fishponds of the county. The three ponds are Pysgodlyn Mawr, Megan Felin and the Warren Mill pond. These ponds are filled with swamp plants and are of great interest to the naturalist. Pysgodlyn Mawr is the only place where the plant *Pilularia globulifera* is found. Much of this area is now given over to forestry and the 'Hensol Forest' was planted in the period 1929 to 1933. The Japanese larch, Norwegian spruce and Corsican pine grown here make excellent pit wood and fencing material. The Forestry Commission nursery at Taironen was started in 1936 and R. E. Pallett was its first Chief Forester. He was in charge of the nursery until the end of the Second World War, by which time it occupied about 100 acres and employed about 150 regular and 40 seasonal workers from the surrounding district. Today the nursery is the forest centre for some 3,000 acres of woodland, which provide direct labour for about 25 men. At the height of its production the nursery provided about 15 million young trees annually for planting out mainly in the Welsh forests.

The chief building of interest in the little village of Welsh St. Donats is Great House. It was a gentleman's residence in the eighteenth century when it belonged to the Llewellin family, one of whom, John Llewellin, rose to become High Sheriff in 1789. In the last century a noted agriculturalist, W. V. Huntley, who became Secretary of the Glamorganshire General Agricultural Society, lived here for nearly 50 years. Malkin, when he visited Welsh St. Donats in 1803, was most impressed with the Welsh type of pigsty he found standing in the village. He wrote: 'In this village are several specimens of the genuine Welsh pig-sty, the conical form and solid fabric of which give an air of architectural dignity to these edifices, not granted to the habitations of so slovenly a race in England'. The pigsties, however, have alas long since disappeared from the village scene.

PENDOYLAN

THE parish of Pendoylan is situated about seven miles west of Cardiff and contains the most attractive village in the whole of the Border Vale. The village has been awarded the title of the Best Kept Village in Glamorgan in 1958, 1966, 1967 and 1969 as well as the Best Kept Village in Wales in 1967 and 1969. The village comprises a church, a small primary school, a village inn known as the *Red Lion* and about thirty houses. The church, which is dedicated to St Cattwg, is a substantial building in the Norman style and has a massive embattled western tower, which may be late medieval. Other medieval features include the stairs to the rood loft. The church was restored in 1855 and 1893. The inn lies to the south of the churchyard and probably dates from the beginning of the nineteenth century. A post-war housing site has been built south of the inn and forms an attractive and integral part of the existing settlement. Across the road is Great House, the seat of the

Caerwigau Isaf   Photograph: Haydn Baynham

Williams family throughout the eighteenth century. The first village school was built in 1850 by Rowland Fothergill of Hensol Castle until the present school was built in 1873, again by the Fothergill family. In the field opposite the inn are traces of the old cockpit, and there are six almshouses which were built in 1817.

When the Border Vale was conquered by the Normans the greater part of the less attractive soils was left in the hands of the Welsh and only later incorporated into the lordship of Talyfan. But that part of the parish to the south-east of the Caerwigau Mill brook lies on the freely drained soils and was quickly acquired by the Normans and formed part of the fee granted to the de Bonville family. In the twelfth century forty acres at Caerwigau were given to the Templars, who rented it out to the monks of Margam for 3s. 4d. a year. Later the monks acquired further property in this area and erected a chapel at Caerwigau. By the early fourteenth century Griffith Fawr, a descendant of Iestyn ap Gwrgant, the last prince of Glamorgan, lived at Caerwigau and became the founder of a family known as the 'Llewelyn of Caerwigga'. The manor remained in the hands of the Llewelyn family for hundreds of years and the old manor house of Caerwigau Isaf was built during the Tudor period.

The fine, castellated mansion of Hensol, now used as a mental hospital, is easily the largest house in the parish. As far back as the reign of Charles II it had as many as eighteen hearths and must have been one of the largest houses in the Border Vale at that time. The early history of Hensol is rather obscure, but it is mentioned in a deed of 1429 in the Talbot of Hensol collection in the National Library of Wales, in which Griffith Fychan ap Griffith ap Llywelyn of Hensol grants his lands in Talygarn, Talyfan, and Llwyn Rhyddid to his son Hywel ap Griffith. They are possibly the ancestors of Richard Thomas of Pendoylan and his son Jenkin ap Richard who feature in another deed relating to the Hensol property in 1556. Jenkin ap Richard was the father of Judge David Jenkins, 1582-1663, whom we have already mentioned. The Jenkins' of Hensol were great patrons of Welsh literature and music and Richard Jenkins, the son of the Judge, was a well known harpist in his day. The mansion and estate were acquired in the eighteenth century by the Talbots, through the marriage of Charles Talbot with the Jenkins heiress, Cecil Mathew of Castell-y-Mynach. Charles Talbot was Lord Chancellor of England from 1733 to 1737 and was created 'Lord Talbot of Hensol'. At the close of the eighteenth century the Talbots left Hensol and the castle was bought by Samual Richardson, a noted agriculturalist. He made great improvements in land drainage and introduced the threshing machine to replace the old flail method of extracting the seed from the corn. Richardson sold the castle in 1815 to Benjamin Hall, the son-in-law of Richard Crawshay of Cyfarthfa. Hall was the first of the Welsh iron-masters to enter politics and he bought Hensol at a cost of £45,000 to enhance his social position in the county. His son was Sir Benjamin Hall of 'Big Ben' fame who spent much of his childhood at Hensol. The estate then passed to William Crawshay of Cyfarthfa, who greatly enlarged and altered Hensol in 1835 making it into the 'mock Gothic' place that we see today. In 1839 it was sold to Rowland Fothergill, the Aberdare iron-master, and the Fothergills and their successors, the Prices, remained there until 1926 when it was purchased by the Glamogan County Council for use as a mental hospital.

PONTYCLUN AND DISTRICT

PONTYCLUN is a nineteenth century industrial creation around a railway station. Before the construction of the South Wales Railway in 1850 it was literally no more than a bridge over the River Clun and an old farmhouse called Pontyclun Fawr close by. The only sizeable community in the district was Miskin which was then called New Mill. Talbot Green did not exist, and at Brynsadler there was only a chapel and a single cottage on the Llanharry road junction. The name 'Pontyclun' did not come into official use until 1893. Earlier records give the name in various forms including 'Clune' in 1205, 'Cloune' in 1280, 'Pont Gloun' in 1536 and 'Pontyclown' in 1732. The latter spelling probably influenced the name 'Pontyclown' to be used by the Post Office to frank letters and parcels from about 1881. Until a few years ago the older inhabitants still pronounced the place as 'Pontyclown', but nowadays everyone uses the form 'Pontyclun'.

As a result of the construction of the South Wales railway a small village was built on the north side of the line roughly where the *Windsor Arms* is today. Two of the earliest streets to be built were School Street and Llantrisant Road. The most rapid growth of Pontyclun occurred a few years later once Pontyclun had become an important railway centre with extensions from the main line to the Rhondda Valley, Pontypridd and Cowbridge. After 1870 a number of new industries were established in close proximity to the

Cowbridge Road, Pontyclun, in the early 1900s

Llantrisant Road, Pontyclun, at the turn of the century

A 1930s excursion party on Pontyclun station platform

135

railway. The Ely Tin Plate Works, the Ely Steam Joinery, Messrs Noel Ltd., and the Llantrisant Gas Works as well as the traditional industries of iron and coal attracted to the area a large number of work-people who settled at Pontyclun and the surrounding villages.

Religious and social amenities were soon provided and among the first were the erection of several nonconformist chapels, the earliest of which was Bethel Baptist Church founded in 1876. A National School was opened in School Street in 1878 and Anglican services were also held there until St. Paul's Church was built in 1895 at a cost of £1,600. As the population of the village increased it became necessary to build an iron school during the years of the First World War. About 1870 the *Windsor Arms* and the *Bute Hotel* were built. The original *Bute* had stood near the site of St. Paul's Church, but the licence was transferred at this time to the present inn.

Pontyclun station has been closed since 1964. Yet in its heyday it was always a hive of activity, especially during the two World Wars. During the First World War trains carrying coal from the Rhondda Valley to Portsmouth and Southampton hurried through the station. Huge crowds of holiday makers from the valleys poured into Pontyclun on their way to the Pant races or a day of picnicing on Maesyfelin fields. And in the last war many munition workers travelled by rail to factories at Treforest and Bridgend. Many of the trains were manned by Pontyclun men and some of the early train drivers on the Taff Vale railway were remarkable characters. Henry Hake of Pantyquesta was one of them. Henry liked his ale and because he would only get home at weekends he would spend all Saturday night drinking. Near Pantyquesta farm where Henry lived was a spring of very cold, clear water. Henry's routine on the morning after his drinking bout was to go down to this spring to drink several jugs of water which always had a beneficial effect on his hangover. He would then return to the farm house where he would throw a huge steak on to the open fire until it was cooked and then with his bare hands pick it off and devour it.

Throughout the early years of the present century, Pontyclun continued to expand, but it was felt that the growing community sorely needed a social and cultural centre. Accordingly, the local squire of Talygarn, Godfrey Clark, built the Pontyclun Institute in 1910 and bowls, tennis and indoor sporting facilities were provided but no liquor was allowed. The Institute proved an immediate attraction and over 300 members availed themselves of the club's facilities. Soon afterwards the First World War broke out and the building was adapted for use as an Army Hospital. The Institute prospered during the Second World War mainly because of the influx into the area of handsomely-paid American soldiers, but in

136

Army hospital at Pontyclun Institute , 1916

the lean times of the post-war era, it was nearly forced to close. In 1958, however, it was decided that the rugby, soccer and cricket clubs of the district should combine under a single roof and for the Institute to be replaced by a comprehensive Athletic Club. Much credit is due to the original management committee of Alby Davies, Bill West, Len Ray, Price Williams, Randall Probin, Ernie Trott, Ron Leek, George Grimes and Ron Kempster whose early efforts ensured the ultimate success of the venture. Today, the Athletic Club has over 1,000 members and offers a full range of sporting and recreational facilities.

Pontyclun Rugby Football Club can be justly proud of their traditions. The club is one of the oldest in Wales and was founded as far back as 1886. Their membership of the W.R.U. dates from 1897 and their reputation over the years has been very much in keeping with their proud history. During the 1920's the team was known as the 'Lilywhite's' and at that time one street — Loftus Terrace — supplied almost a whole team to the Club each Saturday. With players like Reg, Tom and Bert Ferris, Jackie Waters, John Holmes, Jack Thomas, John Trask, the Shufflebotham lads (Jack, Martin, Fred and Wallace), Edgar Reeves, Bill Long, Val Shaw, Jack Harris and Billy Star, it was no wonder they called the street 'Hell Fire Row'. The most impressive season was in 1928-29 when the Club won all its home matches and never allowed the opponents to cross the line. A film was made of the achievements of this famous side by Phil Phillips, a local cinema owner, and it must be among the most fascinating of the early records of the game in Wales. The team played on the Mill Field, where the Pant School is now located and for years changed in the *Windsor Arms*. It was during the twenties that Pontyclun produced its finest

Pontyclun R.F.C. of the late 1920s

player T. E. Rees, nicknamed 'Tommy Italy' because his father had gone to Italy to assist in the tin-plate industry. Tommy Rees has been described as one of the best fullbacks of his time. He played for London Welsh and was capped four times for Wales against Ireland, France, New South Wales and England during the years 1926 to 1928. At the peak of his footballing career he went north and signed as a professional with Oldham. He played for Great Britain in Rugby League in 1929 and became a Rugby League referee after the War. The post-war years were lean and chairman Tom Anstee and secretary Jack Cox found it difficult to keep the club solvent. However, in 1956 a fine team came to the fore and was a perfect blend of youth and experience. Youngsters like Roy Charles, J. Hurley, J. Barnes, Tony Foyle, Allan Perret, David Jenkins and Trevor Smith combined under the captaincy of Bryn Rees with experienced players like Hubert Burridge, Howard Thomas, Ron Roberts, Billy Martin, L. Russell, K. Parsons and D

Rugger star Cliff Jones, one of Wales' outstanding outside halves in the 1930s. Capped 13 times 1933-38. A senior vice-president of the W.R.U. and the senior selector with more than 15 years' service

Doble to make a fine team who were a force to be reckoned with for several seasons. By this time Cliff Jones, the famous Welsh international, had become President of the club. Cliff, the son of a well known Rhondda public figure Councillor Dan Jones, J.P., played thirteen times for Wales between 1933 and 1938, and was captain of the side throughout the 1938-9 season. He was one of the greatest outside halves of all time. After the War he developed into one of the leading administrators of the game, especially in the sphere of selection and coaching. Towards this end he joined the Welsh Rugby Union in 1956 as a Vice-President and has been a member of the Big Five ever since. He has been the Chairman of the Big Five on four occasions and its convenor for seven years. He has sat on the Sports Council for Great Britain and helped in the formation of a separate Sports Council for Wales. On settling in Pontyclun Cliff Jones has witnessed the building up of a rugby stronghold in this fast-growing community, with special emphasis being placed on mini-rugby. A tournament attracting young schoolboys from as far afield as Carmarthen and London Welsh is now held annually at Pontyclun. In 1964 Hedley Benyon initiated a successful youth section and the club's sevens tournament is one of the oldest in the country.

Sport apart, Pontyclun has always enjoyed a vigorous social life and many of the older inhabitants still recall the delightful hours spent at the many fairs and circuses that visited the village, especially those brought by John Studt. He established a show cinema alongside the *Windsor Arms* and later a circuit of three ultra modern cinemas at Pontyclun, Llanharan and Pencoed, which became a source of entertainment to thousands of people before the advent of television. Many people remember following the Wye Valley otter hounds which used to meet outside the *Ivor Arms*, Brynsadler, and hunt the local rivers. A regular visitor to Maesyfelin farm at this time was Madam Clara Novello-Davies the well-known music teacher and conductor. Madam Clara had close links with the Border Vale as her grandfather was William Evans of Ty Fry, Pendoylan. Accompanied by her young son Ivor, she would travel down from Cardiff with her choir to give concerts at Tabernacle Chapel and they always had their tea at Maesyfelin farm.

Over the bridge from Pontyclun lies the modern village of Brynsadler. One of the earliest buildings was Seion Chapel and William Evans of Tonyrefail preached at the opening service in 1830. The *Ivor Arms* was built sometime in the 1860's and for many years the Old Crown Brewery stood opposite it. Many of the inhabitants of Brynsadler are of Cornish origin who came to work in the Mwyndy and Bute iron mines. It is said that they settled at

Brynsadler to be as far away as possible from the Welsh speaking inhabitants of Llantrisant who at first resented their presence in the area. There are two ancient buildings not far from Brynsadler. One is the corn mill called 'Felin Fawr' which belonged to the Marquess of Bute. The other is a farm called Twyll y Cardotyn 'Beggars Deceit', which has a very macabre history indeed. According to the story a feeble old lady, much weakened by the severe weather then prevailing, pleaded with the owner for a night's rest. During the evening the suspicion of a member of the family was aroused and the weather-beaten old crone turned out to be a virile middle-aged man intent on robbing the poor farmer of his half yearly rent. Justice was rough in those days and the imposter was murdered for his deceit.

Not far from Brynsadler, strung out along the Llantrisant to Cowbridge road, lies the expanding residential village of Talygarn. Talygarn mansion is one of the most handsomely decorated houses in the Border Vale. It was rebuilt by George Thomas Clark, the well-known engineer and historian, in the middle of the nineteenth century. Before Clark's time there was a modest mansion on the spot which had been the manor house of the ancient lordship of Talygarn. For many years the house had been in the possession of farmers and had fallen into decay. The previous owner, the Rev. William Lisle, had improved the property and finding the roads in the district unfit for a gentleman's carriage he had them widened and equipped with signposts. He was remarkably eccentric and always kept his room temperature at about 90°. It is said he was a poison specialist who always kept a snake pit in the grounds to

St Ann's Church. Talygarn

house his deadly reptiles. G. T. Clark carried out considerable alterations and extensions before his death in 1898 and his son, Godfrey Clark, completed the task by building the eastern tower. In 1923 Talygarn was purchased by the Miners' Welfare for £20,000, and the house and 140 acres were retained to be used as a Convalescent Home for injured and sick miners. Subsequently it was converted into a Rehabilitation Centre.

Not far from Talygarn mansion stood the ancient Chapel-of-Ease which had been restored by Sir Leoline Jenkins. This was replaced by the Church of St Ann, which was erected in 1887 by G. T. Clark, in memory of his wife Ann, the daughter of Henry Lewis, of Greenmeadow. In conclusion, it can be stated that G. T. Clark and his descendants were model landlords and when his grandson decided to sell the estate all the tenants were given the chance of buying the farms they had rented. Before leaving Brynsadler a brief mention should be made of the United Clubs Brewery which replaced the old Crown Brewery in the post-war period. The company was formed in 1919 by Clubs and Clubmen. In 1954 a new brewery was built at Brynsadler and it employs a large number of men from the immediate locality. The Rosser family from Llanharry has a record number of six brothers employed there. The company at present supplies over 500 clubs in South Wales, Birmingham and the West of England with over 3,000 barrels per week and its main products are Club Pale Ale, Special Best Bitter, Crown Keg and Sovereign Keg. During the last five years the company has experienced substantial growth in the draught lager market, which now accounts for 12% of the total sales. Ceri Evans, the director of the United Clubs Brewery, is justly proud of his product for his S.B.B. won the best-in-show championship cup at the Brewers' Exhibition in 1964.

Talbot Green is situated about a mile north of Pontyclun and owes its importance almost entirely to its position at a cross roads, which enabled it to become a junction for bus services between the Vale and Blaenau. The earliest name for the place was Ton Ysguborau, but a few generations ago it was called Green Talbot. The green stood by the present Post Office and in the middle of it was an old fashioned pump with a hand. Apart from the *Talbot Arms* there were only a few houses, except for a row of cottages near the bus station. These were demolished recently and have been replaced by a modern shopping centre.

The manner in which the place acquired the name Talbot Green is a most interesting one. It seems to have been acquired almost by accident since Frank Reed, an inspector with the former Rhondda Transport Company, used to send in reports using the name Talbot Green by mistake, and it seems his version stuck. Over the years various companies started bus services from the valleys to Cardiff and Bridgend. Among the first were the 'Rhondda Tramways Company' and the 'South Wales Commercial Motors'. These were replaced in later years by the Rhondda Transport Company and the Western Welsh Omnibus Company. All the 'buses in the early days stopped outside the 'Llantrisant Motors' because at that time the present 'bus station was still an orchard with a large wall around it. It was acquired by the Rhondda Transport Co. as late as 1938 and a new station was built on the site. Apart from the regular bus services, John Williams, the well known proprietor of Llantrisant Motors was one of the first to provide the public with a unique form of transport in his 'Maid of the Mountains' charabanc.

Probably because of its central position, many of the old travelling shows found their way to Talbot Green. Freeman's, Wadbrook's, Scarrott's and John Studt's shows attracted large crowds to the fields adjacent to the 'bus station. Opposite the *Talbot Arms* was a Quoit Ground and there was even an Athletic Club in existence in the 1920's. This was supervised by Talbot Green's own strong man, Geoffrey Retter, whose feats of strength are still argued about today. Geoff, a weight-lifting champion, gave many exhibition shows during which he would drive a 6 inch nail into a 3 inch plank of wood with his fist. Another place where the crowds gathered in those days was Moses Bosanko's billiard hall which was an old army hut attached to the Llantrisant Motors.

Miskin was the only community of any size in the vicinity of Pontyclun in the nineteenth century. It was called the village of New Mill and was a small cluster of buildings strung out between

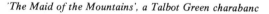

The Maid of the Mountains', a Talbot Green charabanc

Boy scouts at New Mill, Miskin   Photograph: Haydn Baynham

the three-pronged road fork by the present War Memorial and the River Ely. Alongside the river stood the water mill, which was still operating in the early years of the present century. As our picture shows, the mill and its surrounding land is still used today as a Scouts' headquarters. Miskin manor is a nineteenth-century residence built on the old foundations of a Tudor mansion by David Williams 1809-1863, the Welsh coal-owner and eisteddfodwr. The earlier house had belonged to the Bassett family for three centuries and William Bassett, the last of the line, was made High Sheriff of Glamorgan in 1734.

Of the several generations of distinguished members of the Williams' family of Miskin none achieved greater fame than David Williams, who was a typical example of a 'self-made' man of the last century. He was born at Llwyn Drain farm in Ystradowen, but by sheer grit and perseverence rose to a prominent position in the coal mining world of South Wales. He opened collieries at Ynyscynon, Cwm-bach and Aberaman. Later he sunk the Deep Duffryn colliery at Mountain Ash and having successfully won the coal, sold it for the huge sum of £42,000. He bought and sold further pits and attained a great fortune. He never lost touch, however, with the working classes and he spent much time conducting and adjudicating at their local eisteddfodau. He composed much poetry himself and became a popular figure in the literary world of Wales. The movement for the establishment of the National Eisteddfod owes much to his generosity and he was determined to see it held in North and South Wales alternatively. His descendant is Sir Brandon Rhys-Williams, the present owner of Miskin Manor.

143

LIST OF SUBSCRIBERS

Mr & Mrs M. Ainsworth, Brynsadler
Mrs C. L. Ambury, Llanharry
Mr W. Ambury, Llanharry
Mr S. P. Andrew, Welsh St Donats
Mrs C. Andrews, Blaengarw
Mr John A. Andrews, Blaengarw
Mrs N. M. Aston, Pontyclun
Mr Ivor Austin, Cardiff
Mrs Pam Austin, Llanharry
Mr Ray Austin, Llanharry

Mr John Bagg, Pentre Meyrick
Mr B. T. Bailey, Llanharry
Mr Ivor Baker, Llanharry
Mr Wayne Baker, Llanharry
Mrs Gladys Ball, Llanharry
Mrs Marjorie Ball, Bridgend
Misses Michelle and Susan Bartlett, Llantrisant
Miss Linda Beach, Llanharry
Mr Samuel Beach, Llanharan
Mr R. G. Bendle, Pontyclun
Mr & Mrs T. Benjamin, Brynna
Mr & Mrs Peter Bickford, New York, U.S.A.
Mr J. C. Bolt, Talbot Green
Mrs L. Bowden, Llanharry
Mrs T. A. Boyland, Llanharry
Master Andrew Brain, Llanharry
Mr & Mrs Peter Brett, Llanharry
Mr Cyril Brown, Llanillterne
Mr Wm. M. Brydle, Pontyclun
Mrs D. Bugler, Llanharry
Mr C. Bunston, Llanharry

Mr & Mrs R. Campbell, Llanharry
Michael, Denise and Dawn Casley, Llanharry
Mr Gordon Cattell, Llanharry
Mr & Mrs H. Claridge, Llanharry
Mr & Mrs I. K. Claridge, Llanharry
Mr & Mrs M. Clifford, Tonyrefail
Miss K. M. Cocks, Barry
Mr & Mrs Keith Cogbill, Llanharry
Mr Thomas A. Coombs, Brynna
Mr C. Corbett, Llanharry
Mr Jeff Corbett, Llanharry
Mr Gwyn Crandon, Pontyclun
Miss Tracey Cuddihy, Llanharry
Master Simon Cudicio, Llanharry
Mr & Mrs Perce Curnow, Pennington, Australia
Mr & Mrs Alun Dando, Bridgend
Mr & Mrs Mervyn Dando, Llanharry
Mrs M. Dauncey, Llanharry
Dr T. M. Dauncey, Barry
Mr Tony Dauncey, Llanharry
Mr Brian Davies, Llanharry Meadow
Mr & Mrs H. Davies, Fremantle, Australia
Mr Haydn Davies, Porthcawl
Mr Isaac Davies, Llanharry
Mr J. C. Davies, Pontyclun
Mrs Margaret Davies, Llanharry
Mrs Sandra Davies, Bridgend
Councillor Mervyn Davis, Llanharry
Mr Ivor R. Day, B.E.M., Barry
Mr & Mrs E. Deakin, Llanharry
Mr I. Deakin, Llanharry
Mr S. C. Deeley, Trehingyll
Miss L. Demmer, Llanharry
Miss Rhonda Demmer, Llanharry

Miss Susan Demmer, Llanharry
Mr A. Denscombe, Llanharry
Mr L. Denscombe, Llanharan
Mrs Patricia Derrick, Taunton
Mrs Pauline Derrick, Chard
Mrs Pat Devonshire, Llanharry
Mr Eric J. Dew, Litchard
Mrs M. Dingle, Talygarn
Mrs Anne Doble, Llanharry
Mr Anthony Doble, Llanharry
Mr David T. Dodd, Llanharry
Mr Douglas Dulson, Talbot Green
Mrs Vera Dykes, Llanharry
Mr & Mrs W. D. Dykes, Llanharry

Miss B. M. Eden, Llanharry
Mr John Edwards, Coity
Yasmin and Alexander Eley, Llanharry
Mrs Yvonne Eley, Llanharry
Mr W. G. England, Beddau
Mrs M. Enticott, Llanharry
Mr David Evans, Llanharry
Mrs Enid Evans, Llanharry
Mr Gwyn Evans, Llanharry
Mr Islwyn Evans, Llanharry
Mr Leighton L. Evans, Llanharan
Mr Malcolm J. Evans, Llanharry
Mr Steve Evans, Llanharry
Miss Victoria Evans, Llanharry

Mr Cyril Field, Llanharry
Mr Paul Rees Fisher, Pontyclun
Mrs M. E. Fitzgibbon, Llanharry
Mr & Mrs R. J. Fitzgibbon, Llanharry
Mrs Iris Fletcher, Llanharry
Mr Gwyn Floyd, Llanharry
Miss Caroline Julie Francis, Llanharry
Miss Emma Jayne Francis, Llanharry
Miss Gillian Frederick, Llanharry
Mr William Gallagher, Llanharry
Mr Stephen Giles, Llanharry
Mr Steven Golubovic, Llanharry
Claire and Estelle Goodchild, Troes
Mr & Mrs G. Goulden, Llanharry
Mr T. J. Goulden, Talygarn
Miss Margaret Grant, Hanwell, London
Mrs R. Green, Llanharry
Mrs Betty Greenslade, Llanharry
Miss Kay Greenslade, Llanharry
Mr Michael Gregory, Kenfig Hill
Mrs E. Gribble, Llanharry
Mr D. J. Griffin, Llanharry
Donna and Denise Griffin, Llanharry
Mr Neil Griffin, Llanharry
Mrs Len Griffiths, Llanharry
Paul and Sian Griffiths, Llantrisant
Mr T. Griffiths, Llanharry
Debbie, Angela and Paul Groom, Llanharry
Mrs Kathleen Groom, Persondy, St Mary Hill
Mr & Mrs Reg Groom, Llanharry
Mr Robin Gwilliam, Llanharry

Mr & Mrs M. J. Hall, Llanharry
Mr Kenneth Hardiman, Inverness
Miss Angela P. Harris, Pentre Meyrick
Mr David Harris, Pentre Meyrick
Mr George Hart, Llanharry

Mr Ronald Harvey, Pontyclun
Miss Gillian Hawkes, Llanharry
Mr B. R. Hayes, Llansannor
Mr W. Hearse, Llanharry
Mr & Mrs Alan Henderson, Llanharry
Mr Richard Hendrie, Llanharry
Mr & Mrs E. Hill, Bear Cross, Hants.
Mr Howard Hopkins, Ystradowen
Mr B. Howe, Llanharry
Mr Bernard Howells, Llanharry
Mr & Mrs H. Howells, Llanharry
Mr C. Hucker, Llanharry
Master Jason Huggett, Llanharry
Mrs Renee Huggins, Taunton
Master Martin Huish, Llanharry
Mr Peter Hunnisett, Llanharry
Mr K. M. Hutchings, Cowbridge

Mr & Mrs M. Jenkins, Pentre Meyrick
Misses Dawn and Nicola Jobbins, Llanharry
Miss Lynda Jobbins, Llanharry
Bryn John, B.Sc., Ph.D., F.I.Chem. Eng., Michigan, U.S.A.
Mr & Mrs Brynmor John, Llanharan
Mr & Mrs Gareth John, Llanharry
Mrs June John, Llanharry Meadow (2)
Mr & Mrs Keith John, Llanharry
Mrs Andrea Johns, Pontyclun
Mr Barrie Dennis Johns, Llanharan
Mr & Mrs Dennis Johns, Llanharry
Master Gavin Johns, Pontyclun
Mr Robert Johns, Pencoed
Mr Thomas Johns, Llanharan
Mr & Mrs Alec Jones, Llanharry
Mr Derek Jones, Pencoed
Mr Gwynne Jones, Llwynypia
Mair and Paul Jones, Llanharry
Mr Rodney G. Jones, Aberfan
Mrs Sally Jones, Llanharry
Mr Stephen Jones, Llanharry
Mrs J. Jordan, Llanharry
Mrs L. A. Jordan, Llanharan

Mr R. Keay, Llanharry
Mrs Dulcie Kerner, Llanharry
Mrs Maralyn Kimber (nee Morris), Wiltshire
Mr Granville Kinsey, Llanharry

Master Wayne Ivor Lamerton, Brynsadler
Mr James Lamont, Llanharry
Mrs Marlene Lamont, Llanharry
Mrs Esme Lewis, Llanharry
Mrs H. Lewis, Llanharry (2)
Councillor and Mrs Harry Lewis, Llanharry (2)
Mrs J. Lewis, c/o Llanhari Junior School
Mr L. Lewis, Llanharry
Mrs Maureen Lewis, Llanharry
Miss Susan Lewis, Talbot Green
Mr Vernon Lewis, St Mary Hill
  Llanhari County Primary School (2)
Mrs Yvonne Lumsden, Penarth
Mr Brian C. Luxton, B.A., Barry

Mr Christian Martinson, Pencoed
Mrs E. Mason, Llanharry
Councillor and Mrs Brinley Matthews, Llanharry
Mr & Mrs Dewi Matthews, Ystradowen
Mrs Florence Matthews, Llanharry
Mr Michael Mathews, Llantrisant
Mr & Mrs N. Mathias, Llanharry
Donna and Wayne Merry, Llanharry
Councillor and Mrs Ray Milsom, Llanharry Meadow
Miss Amanda Morgan, Llanharry
Mrs Audrey B. Morgan, Llanharry
Mr & Mrs Brian Morgan, Llanharry

Mr & Mrs Hywel Morgan, Wolverhampton
Councillor Marion Morgan, Llanharry
Mr & Mrs William Morris, Llanharry
Mrs Marion Morris, Llanharan
Mr Tony Mott, Llanharry

Mr & Mrs L. E. Newton, Llanharry
Mrs E. Nicholls, Belfast
Mr & Mrs Peter Norfolk, Llanharry

Mr & Mrs Ron Owen, Llanharry

Mr Alan Panting, Llanharry
Carol and Roy Panting, Llanharry
Mr D. Parsons, Llanharry
Mrs Pat Pascoe, Llanharry
Pauline, Beverley and Ceri Pascoe, Llanharry
Mr & Mrs K. B. Perkins, Llanharry
Mr Christopher Pick, Llanharry
Mr Ken Pick, Llanharry
Les, Gwyneth and Rachel Pick, Llanharan
Mr A. E. Pickard, B.A., Bondi Junction, Australia
Mr & Mrs Lyn Ponting, Llanharry
Shellie, Julia and Joanne Povey, St Nicholas
Mr S. Powell, Llanharry
Mrs Thelma Powell, Llanharry
Mr & Mrs Wilf Powell, Llanharry
Mrs Elizabeth Rosa Pratt, Trerhingyll
Mr Keith Price, Llanharry
Mr & Mrs Len Pring, Llanharry
Mrs M. Pring, Llanharry

Mr Elved Radcliffe, Rhoose
Mr & Mrs Maurice Randall, Llanharry (2)
Mr Clifford William Rawle, Pontyclun
Mr & Mrs Cecil Rees, Llanharry
Mr E. J. Rees, Llanharry
Mr Graham Rees, Aberkenfig (2)
Mr Martin Rees, Llanharry
Mrs M. Rees, Llanharry
Mrs Margaret Rees, Ty Candy Farm, St Mary Hill
Mr W. Trevor Rees, Coity
Mr E. Reeves, Pontyclun
Mr & Mrs K. Reeves, Llanharry
Mrs Gladys Reynolds, Chingford
Mrs Pat Roberts, Medina, Australia
Mr Wayne A. Roberts, Llanharry
Mr William Roberts, Llantrisant
Mrs Joan Robson, Ashbury, Wiltshire
Master Richard Rogers, Llanharry
Mr & Mrs Edgar Rosser, Llanharry
Mr & Mrs Mervyn Rosser, Llanharry
Neil, Nigel and Julie Rossiter, Llanharry
Mr Brian Russell, Llanharry
Mr & Mrs R. Russell, Llanharry
Mr & Mrs D. B. Ryan, Llanharry

Mr & Mrs Dilwyn Scourfield, Llanharry
Mr & Mrs John Scourfield, Nantymoel
Dr Himadri Seth, Pontyclun
Mr & Mrs Des Sharkey, Llanharry
Mr Val Shaw, Llanharry
Miss E. Shell, Llanharan
Mr George and Councillor G. S. Shuttleworth, Llanharry
Mrs B. Slade, Llanharry
Mr Colin Smith, Llanharry
Mr John Smith, Llanharry
Mrs Margaret Smith, Llanharry
Mr R. M. Smith, Talbot Green
Mr & Mrs A. E. Sparks, Pencoed
Mr Reg Stevens, Llanharry
Miss Sara Stevens, Talbot Green
Mr Leighton Stone, Kenfig Hill
Mr & Mrs P. Stone, Llanharry

145

Mr & Mrs W. L. Stone, Pencoed
Mr Douglas Summers, Llanharry
Mr Henry Skevington Summers, Llanharry
Miss Pauline Summers, Llanharry
Mr Ray Summers, Llanharry

Mr Brian Taylor, Llantrisant
Mrs H. Taylor, Bryncethin
Mr R. T. and Mrs J. D. M. Taylor, Talbot Green
Mr David J. Thomas, Llanharry
Mrs Fleur Thomas, Llanharry
Mr Goronwy Thomas, Pencoed
Miss Jean Thomas, Llanharry
Mr Kenneth Thomas, Llanharry
Mr Llew Thomas, Llanharry
Peter Thomas, M.D., Llysworney (2)
Mr Phillip G. Thomas, Ty Candy Farm, St Mary
  Hill
Mr Reginald G. Thomas, Llanharry
Mr Robert Thomas, Ash Grove, Llanharry
Mr Robert Thomas, Station Terrace, Llanharry
Mr Robert Thomas, Pencoed
Mr & Mrs Roy Thomas, Pencoed
Mr S. P. Thomas, Llanharry
Mr & Mrs Stuart Thomas, Llanharry
Master Tony Thomas, Llanharry
Mr William Thomas, Llanharry
Mr Mark Thornton, Pontyclun
Mr & Mrs J. D. Timothy, Pontyclun
Mr H. J. Tooze, Llanharry
Mr Howel G. Townsend, Llanharry
Mr Peter Lloyd Townsend, c/o Brynna School

Mrs Irene Vowles, Llanharry
Mr & Mrs J. Vowles, Llanharry

Mr & Mrs D. Wallis, Trerhingyll
Anne and John Warmingham, Llanharry
Mr G. Warner, Llanharry

Mrs D. Warwick, Llanharry
Mr E. Way, Llanharry
Mr Oliver Way, Llanharry
Mr & Mrs Walter Weaver, Llanharry
Mr W. Webb, Pencoed
Mr Cyril Welsh, Llanharan
Mr & Mrs Jeff Welsh, Llanharry
Mr & Mrs Michael Welsh, Caerphilly
Mr Stan Welsh, Llanharry (2)
Mr Vivian G. Welsh, Llanharry
Mr N. Whitton, Llanharry
Mr Robert Whitton, Llanharry
Mrs Betty Williams (nee Rosser), Llanharry
Mr Colin Williams, Llanharry
Mr D. G. Williams, Bridgend
Mr D. L. Williams, Pencoed
Mr Elvet Williams, Llanharry
Mr & Mrs Frank Williams, Llanharry
Mr & Mrs Gary Williams, Llanharry
Councillor Ivor J. B. Williams, Llanharry
Mrs Kay Williams, Llanharry
Mrs Marjorie Shuttleworth Williams, Llanharry
Mr & Mrs R. Williams, Llanharry
Miss Rebecca Williams, Llantrisant
Mr & Mrs Rhys Williams, Llanharry
Miss Sharon Williams, Llanharry
Miss Sian Williams, Llanharry
Mr & Mrs Terry Williams, J.P., Llanharan
Mr W. C. Williams, Llanharan
Mr & Mrs David Wills, Llanharry
Mr Stan Wills, Llanharan
Mr Simon Wintle, Llanharry
Mrs Buddug Witts, Llanharan
Mr Frank Witts, Llanharan
Mr Harry Wood, Litchard
Mr T. Worgan, Llanharry
Mr Andrew Wride, Llanharry
Mr Percival Wright, Pontyclun